THE OLD MAN AND THE SEA

Also by Anthony Smith

Blind White Fish in Persia
Sea Never Dry
High Street Africa
Throw Out Two Hands
The Body (also titled *The Human Body*)
The Dangerous Sort
The Seasons
Mato Grosso
Beside The Seaside
Wilderness
A Persian Quarter Century
A Sideways Look
The Mind
Smith & Son
The Great Rift: Africa's Changing Valley
Explorers of the Amazon
The Free Life
Survived!
Ballooning
The Weather
Lost Lady Of The Amazon

THE OLD MAN AND THE SEA

Anthony Smith

Constable • London

CONSTABLE

First published in Great Britain in 2015 by Constable

Copyright © Anthony Smith, 2015

The moral right of the author has been asserted.

Extract taken from 'East Coker' taken from *Four Quartets* © Estate of
T.S. Eliot and reprinted by permission of Faber and Faber Ltd

A CIP catalogue record for this book
is available from the British Library.

ISBN 978-1-47211-521-8 (hardback)
ISBN 978-1-47212-002-1 (trade paperback)
ISBN 978-1-47211-531-7 (ebook)

Typeset in Baskerville by Photoprint, Torquay
Printed and bound in Great Britain by CPI Group (UK) Ltd, Croydon, CR0 4YY

Constable
is an imprint of
Constable & Robinson Ltd
100 Victoria Embankment
London EC4Y 0DY

An Hachette UK Company
www.hachette.co.uk

www.constablerobinson.com

Old men ought to be explorers
Here or there does not matter
We must be still and still moving
Into another intensity
For a further union, a deeper communion
Through the dark cold and the empty desolation,
The wave cry, the wind cry, the vast waters
Of the petrel and the porpoise.

from 'East Coker', *Four Quartets* by T. S. Eliot

Foreword

All I knew for sure was that Day Ninety of our venture had turned into quite the most hazardous and unsettling of them all. A storm had caused us to lose control, utterly and totally alarmingly. We were powerless, unable to tie down our flapping sail around any form of cleat. It was also dark and there was heavy rain. Of greatest concern were the reefs that lay downwind, with all their magnificent beauty now transformed into vicious realms of rock. Each piece of nearby land was protected by coral bulwarks far more effective than any battlement. What would happen to our craft should we collide with such a defensive bastion? Or rather what would happen to those of us onboard because collision with these reefs was about to become a frightening certainty.

For my part I sat in the cabin watching all the instruments. These told me, in a cold-blooded manner, what I already knew. We were less than a mile from a Bahamian island, with wind and wave doing their damnedest to unite the two of us. As for the quantity of reef lying immediately ahead that might keep us separate, it was in possession of an appetite for on-site destruction far greater than that of mere wave or sandy beach.

Our clever software was most precise with its information, helping me to calculate the interval of time before raft and reef might meet. I even said out loud, 'Ten more minutes,' as if the others onboard had not reached more or less the same conclusion. My companions preferred to stay outside the single cabin, and were silent with their thoughts. Two of them were busily inflating the little dinghy we possessed, a somewhat desperate measure because the thing would be valueless in the storm, and even more so upon a reef as it would surely be shredded instantly. People often like to be doing things if things are being done to them, and in any case pumping with bellows may do no good but also did no harm. I do not know if they even heard my shouts – 'Five more minutes, or maybe four,' 'Two more at the most,' 'Any moment now.'

What a noise there would be! What a terrible sound would come from down below and what destruction would ensue! The instruments would become somewhat pointless and both dinghy pumpers would give up their self-appointed task. Instead those two individuals would surely stand up to concentrate on the hammerings happening all about them.

Was this how our raft would end its days? And was it also how the group of us would reach the conclusion of our lives, with dreadful bangs rather than any kind of whimper? We should have been filming this powerful happening, but were doing nothing of the sort. Why film one's end for others to observe? In fact why do anything, save stay more or less where unhappy legs had taken us? And wonder how on earth, and why on earth, we had reached such a definite predicament.

At all our endings, so they say, our lives will flash before us, and bits of mine certainly did. I do not crave misadventure, but in a long life it has come my way many times. What I have relished are novel experiences, seeing the world from different vantage points and rejoicing in their varied excellence. Even getting out of a crowded bus far from home can be one such form of novelty. There is then a different feel to the air, along with different sounds and smells. No harm usually comes with such simple alterations, however there can be greater hazard if the desire for novelty leads one to embrace a change not normally encountered.

Flying by gas balloon must be fun, I had reasoned to myself a long time ago. It could also be terrifying, and decidedly so when one's fear threatens to gain the upper hand. At 9,000 feet above the Ngong hills of central Kenya, I had no sand remaining in the sacks around my feet. This meant a lethal landing unless magic intervened.

Happily, magic did just that, by selecting a perfect tree, thorny to the hilt and rich with brittle branches, to soften my re-arrival upon the ground where I more properly belonged. That single tree, much damaged by the balloon's abrupt invasion, then discarded our wicker basket towards a neighbouring tree, thus causing all momentum to vanish along with all the fear.

I had thought balloons ideal for seeing the world more properly and gazing upon it pleasingly without either disturbance or having to lift one's feet. I had realized how very wrong I was when mayhem intervened – even more acutely, as that same balloon had been poised between a massive caustic lake (with the potential to blind) and a thundercloud cavorting at up to 50,000 feet (which could kill, and kill rather more than once).

I had also learned that airships can inject another kind of terror, also as antidote to some perfection recently enjoyed. I had relished an airship's ability to stop in the air, with the engine's thrust precisely matching whatever breeze there was, enabling me to gaze upon small deer strolling along the lines of corn, at rabbits thumping their alarm or merely at fish, which are always so much more visible when seen from up above. Should the wind then choose to alter these intensities of joy, I found the craft could change in an instant from stationary to galloping – or so it seemed – thus altering the idyll of a lifetime into a desperate wish to preserve that life just a little longer. Soon, there was an oak tree straight ahead and a sudden rasping of airship rope against leaf profusion, with too much occurring in too short a time before an immediate and ungainly collision with a field of cabbages.

I still have no idea why or how yet another airship on another day had let me live, after its automatic blow-off valves had omitted to accomplish the only task they were ever asked to do. This failure had caused the gas-filled shape above my head to feel almost solid, and therefore poised for a catastrophic burst, but somehow it did not rend itself in two, and even let me escape to walk upon a simple and most attractive field somewhere in Buckinghamshire. Yes, I did kiss its soil, with an ardent fervour that no lady ever received – after all, near-death experiences are not (usually) expected when merely expressing love.

When I rode a motorbike from toe to top of Africa, and then achieved the converse very much later, it was the continent that I wished to see, from near at hand, in all its vast variety. I certainly had no desire to finish all my onboard drink, to feel my tongue grow larger and care not a scrap that I also had no food. It is liquid the body then desires more than anything else – by far. When thirst has been satisfied, perhaps 250 miles further on at the next filling station, hunger can also return and demand proper attention.

Intensities do come thick and fast, following both good or feeble planning, and I have had a feast of them. They cannot be anticipated but are certainly noticed and then merrily treasured if partnered by an exuberant and happy outcome.

I do not court danger; far from it. To go bungee-jumping or playing chicken across railway tracks strikes me as idiotic behaviour. On the other hand it is silly to refrain from some activity merely because it is possible that 'things' might go wrong. The statistics concerning accidents reveal that they take place in the most unlikely of settings, such as the home and even the bedroom. One's own dwelling is probably piped with electricity and gas, of which both are capable of malfunction. The dwelling may have two storeys or even more, and altitude always creates an extra hazard. In short, life itself can be a tricky business, with our beloved motorcar leading to quite substantial mayhem. Within the UK, most deaths linked to such vehicles affect individuals who were not even in them at the time.

To travel by sea may seem perilous at times but those of us onboard the raft had taken great care – which is more than many people do on normal days. We just knew there would be joy in great measure, and this aspect we had embraced as best we could.

When old age arrives, or even the realization that there is more life behind than there is ahead, the suspicion can grow that all intensity might have diminished beyond recall. That, I now know, is not the case. With my ailing body, its frailty much worsened by a motoring accident (which forced a careless driver to pull me from beneath his vehicle), the possibilities of new experience seemed to have quite vanished, but not a bit of it. I had thought that rafting, that mere drifting with whatever wind and current had to offer, might be a gentle activity, particularly with a chair onboard from which to watch the huge wet world go by. It seemed silly and inadequate to travel the Thames, or even the Mississippi as Tom Sawyer and friends had chosen to do, but the Atlantic loomed as both intriguing and exciting. And that was how I eventually found myself with those reefs looming straight ahead, with their ability to destroy every invader of their realm.

T. S. Eliot – at the end of his *Four Quartets* – wrote extraordinarily that 'Old men ought to be explorers'. I, having reached my ninth decade, have had to accept a certain seniority, but rejoiced on reading his words. They almost suggested life onboard a raft, with 'the wave cry, the wind cry' when upon the vast waters 'of the petrel and the porpoise'. It was occasion, he added, for further intensities, with that splendid word so summing up my lifelong desire to go slightly further, to add experience, to encounter novelty, and thereby treasure the planet in yet another way. Surely there would be intensities when crossing the Atlantic upon a bed of pipes and a deck of planks. And being out of touch with the ordinary world. And consuming such a quantity of time, which would surely be partnered by a feast and magnificence of new happenings.

These certainly came our way right from the very start, long before that final day when we had lost control. Yes, we did hit the reef, and did suffer, but I think the greatest fears arrived at the start. And that is where this story most properly begins.

1

The Atlantic's 3,000-mile width lay all ahead when – one mile beyond the peaceful security of the harbour wall – our towing boat discarded the connecting length of rope. At that precise and positive moment all fears bounded with the realization that nothing and no one would then help us. We four on board – me, David Hildred, Andy Bainbridge and John Russell – with a total age of 258 years, would have to navigate and survive as we alone thought fit. There would be storm and squall, almost certainly, together with perils unforeseen as we travelled west for however long the journey took. We had food and water, but also zero knowledge of how the raft would fare, or how we ourselves would fare on the object we had made with pipes, with planks, and ropes, with tautened widths of webbing pulled tight by ratcheting. Would the central cabin be able to withstand undoubted battering from the sea? Would the single sail and single mast perform satisfactorily, even if we did not really know what satisfaction meant? And how would we four get on while living so very cheek by jowl for such a quantity of time? The Atlantic experience would assuredly be fascinating, but its joy might be diminished, or even vanished, by people proximity. And by our sodden clothing, along with a growing realization that rafting and its intensities might not be the perpetual ecstasy of earlier imaginings.

There were also other worries at that time, such as the Spanish inability to give us permission to depart from their Canary island La Gomera. We certainly wondered if – or when – some official craft might arrive to tow us back again to Valle Gran Rey. What ignominy and misery that would be, even if they just took – and then perhaps imprison – the leader of this wayward enterprise, the one whose dream would become more like a nightmare when the venture came to pass. The Spanish were not being difficult. They were following their law stating that novel sea-going craft had to be examined and approved each step of the way. Were our pipes sufficiently strong? What about our central dwelling place and every single rope? The British let everyone go, even in a bath tub, provided they had paid a small price for a name, but woe betide them if help becomes necessary. The authorities do not look kindly at ventures considered fatuous should they get into trouble and officialdom is then happy to pass on bills. We had no wish to annoy the Spanish or to cancel the voyage before it had even begun. Perhaps blind eyes would be turned our way? Perhaps we should do the same? Who knew what was for the best, for I certainly did not.

I, also paymaster, had run out of funds during the final days and we had left with bills unpaid. What might my creditors be doing or proposing now that their bird had flown?

That bird was currently lying damp on a bunk while nursing a miserable infection. I harboured yet more doubts, some reasonable and others possibly idiotic, such as the thought of killer whales slithering onboard to pick us off, or creating waves to wash us off, much as they do with seals on ice. Worry is not a finite business. It can grow and become an amalgam of concerns, each causing internal tightening around one's abdomen, with every form of unhappiness wishing to be heard – and felt.

My crew were not tried or tested friends but brand-new acquaintances. Earlier in this enterprise, when hoping to recruit companions, I had welcomed the thought of pensioners. I wished to assert – as major reason for the voyage – that the elderly could still be enterprising, however past their prime. When I'd gathered my first quartet, I certainly hoped this lively, modestly ancient, varied and distinctive group would lead to suitable sponsors – but not a bit of it.

'You will surely fail,' explained these different kinds of individual.

'Why will we surely fail?'

'Because you are old, that's why.'

I was therefore hoist by the very petard I had been promoting, and I had to let the idea go and look for younger companions (although not too young). Pensioners can be fit and well but in the minds of sponsors and other commentators, plainly disadvantageous for the calendar years each had consumed. The aged, it would seem, should attend coffee mornings, discuss church roofs, visit the local supermarket only at the quietest times, dead-head roses, take mouthfuls of obligatory pills and hope that at least one offspring would get in touch that month. In particular the old should not affirm their demented state by extolling daft ideas, these partnered by pig-headed intent to make them happen.

I, the oldest of the eventual quartet and halfway through my ninth decade, had received much talk of this nature. It was even suggested by various friends that I too should potter with make-believe busyness, thus killing time before time itself killed me.

'Nothing wrong with pottering,' many people said. 'No harm done that way.'

At the back of the raft project was determination to carry on living much as I had always done. Why should I do nothing merely because some 25,000 days had already been consumed?

Much of my life had involved projects, either big or small. These had dictated where my energy, money and time should go. In general I had welcomed these exploits and saw no reason why such antics should come to a sudden stop. Was not a raft eminently suitable for an ancient body, its fundamental simplicity creating the most basic form of travel? With earlier ventures there had generally been some gain along with any problems that had arisen, the fear and weariness, the cost and concern.

During student days (for complicated reasons) I had spent a terrifying time deeply within the displeasing underground canals in Iran, called *qanats*, which were allegedly home to interesting fish. The things proved to possess nothing of the kind but that modest fact did not prevent me from writing a book entitled *Blind White Fish in Persia*. Then came the motorbike trip from Cape Town to Cairo (causing each kidney to object), the ballooning to a host of extraordinary destinations (these never forgotten afterwards), the airshipping to grassy spaces ripe for landing (or cabbages in Bedfordshire) before steamboating on aluminium canoes down 2,000 miles of an Amazonian river. I had also motorbiked back to Cape Town twenty-eight years after the first trip with that bike, hoping to meet again the eager salesman of 1955 and request some money back due to certain deficiencies with my twice-used machine. (Alas, his little shop had become a skyscraper in the interim.)

When advanced years came my way the raft did seem ideal. Gentle and not too arduous – no forest landings, no hefty sandbags, no Brussels sprouts (as the cabbages proved, more expensively, to be), no bowsawing of tropical ironwoods to fuel a hungry boiler and no corrugated highways pummelling two ancient frames, one made from tubular steel and one, in me, from bone. On a raft I could just sit, watch the Atlantic world on every side, think new thoughts, enjoy the scenery, try to

4

reduce the number of my concerns, hope companionship would not prove overwhelming and wonder where (and how and when) the journey might end.

Worry, as I already knew, never vanishes absolutely. It can even increase with greater knowledge. I remember, after a spell of flying, looking at the few bolts which hold a Tiger Moth's wings in place. I dislike even seeing the underside of my car when it's jacked up high, and of course I now remembered with considerable anxiety how various friends and the brand-new crew – inexperts at raft building, every one – had bound the raft's many pipes together, how the decking had been lashed before being screwed in place, and how our 'pig ark' of a cabin had been built and fixed. It was mainly gravity which held the mast in place, or so it had appeared when meanly proffering one euro coin (in lieu of customary and traditional gold) to reside beneath the stepping.

When we were at sea, I became less concerned about Spanish authority as their area of jurisdiction began to vanish in our wake. But still, during those earliest rafting hours, my ancient head stayed clogged, not just with the foul phlegm that colds induce but with anxieties still remaining. Creditors do not worry about boundaries drawn on maps, or varying areas of jurisdiction, and would continue to pursue wherever I happened to be. Neither do whales, whether with the name of killer or something more benign. Such huge animals can, and do, upset sailing craft, merely it would sometimes seem for the hell of it, or for an itch – yes, just there – that had been vexing for several thousand miles. I hoped that sargasso seas would not ensnare, and that storms would gyrate elsewhere when revolving depressingly after some high had become a low. Would we rafters fall apart, fall in or fall foul of each other? Who knew, but the 3,000 miles in front would surely tell. By the third day we had logged less than 100 of them, and it was on that Day Three when my frame was still firmly bunk-borne that I suddenly heard a shout.

'Rudder's broken,' yelled someone from somewhere at the stern.

'So what?' I muttered to myself, there being no space for novel anxiety.

A famous Gary Larsen *Far Side* cartoon shows a schoolroom of pupils with one of them, visibly not the brightest of the bunch, asking to be taught no more because his 'brain was already full'. My mucus-infested and worry-laden head entirely sympathized. The others reported that I had often cried 'Oh, no!' when either in deep sleep or within the shallower kind, and they had asked what in particular had been troubling me. In truth I had no idea. Now, all those severe and numerous concerns – Spain, Debts, Construction, Storm, Personnel, Navigation, Health, Age, Big Mammals, Helplessness – seemed more than adequate to keep it occupied, and there was no room for Rudder. The raft was bouncing up and down haphazardly, as did seem reasonable in that circumstance, and the other members of the crew were soon examining the break while I, with sodden clothing and lying prone, was plainly not in charge of the project I had initiated, and had funded, and was called Captain.

'AM IN MARKET HARBOROUGH STOP WHERE OUGHT I TO BE QUERY' as G. K. Chesterton had – allegedly – once telegrammed his wife in London.

'AM BOUNCING DAMPLY ON A RAFT WITH ATLANTIC STRAIGHT AHEAD STOP HOW COME QUERY' How come indeed? For the moment, with my eighty-four-year-old body in disarray and its head obscenely bunged, I thought somewhat casually about the venture and certainly about the rudder. How would we navigate? Would this breakage truly cause an ending to our voyage? Oh well, I thought, and for the time being, I will dry out these clothes of mine merely by wearing them, pull up a cushion to ease an overloaded skull and wonder what the future has in store. Balloonists revel in the 'unknown destinations' which lie ahead of them. Rafting, as I realized, is much the same. Take off, be towed from port, be abandoned and then wonder what on earth will happen next. Or on ocean, as we chanced to be.

The most amazing fact, which steadily sank into the four of us, was our raft's ability to head downwind even after the rudder break. Of course we had argued where the mast should be, where our single sail should be, and where the cabin should be located (which served, with its bulk, as another form of sail) but we had no prior knowledge of the raft's behaviour once all the decisions had been made. Would it crab sideways, and very awkwardly? Or have a tendency to gyrate, with its prow then favouring all points of the compass seemingly haphazardly? We had not known; we had merely hoped. The fact that those hopes had turned into actuality was quite astonishing. At whatever angle we set the sail, our apex pointed forwards as if some engine was at the rear and driving us in that direction. It was amazing, or even miraculous, and took years off my actual age.

'You lucky bastard,' I even said internally.

The joy was paramount. Nevertheless, the Atlantic was no modest entity. It was enormous and no kind of pond, as it's named so frequently. We had achieved some fifty miles a day, a sizeable daily distance for mere pedestrians. This progress was marked upon our chart and immediately looked pathetic. Divide 50 into 3,000 and the answer is a considerable quantity of time and days. What about the occasions when winds might blow contrarily or the currents misbehave? This was an ocean that we wished to cross, a great body of water, a very lonely place particularly should trouble come our way.

I had once written a book about a friend's faulty pigheadedness. His enthusiasm for crossing the Atlantic by

balloon had led to his downfall and also to the death of everyone onboard. He should never have departed. That was
obvious to those of us who subsequently picked over the details
of his preparations. The balloon was wrong, its capsule was
wrong, and bad weather had made certain that failure came
his way. His departure had been encouraged by the coopera-
tion he had received, the loan of everything he had desired,
the overriding friendliness of everyone who then had watched
him go. Such pressure had helped to cause the end of him,
not intentionally but as assuredly as stabbing him to death.

I too had often felt pressure all around and had pretended
it was not there. There is also pressure from within, this being
no less powerful in urging fulfilment of any enterprise. In
theory a body should be looking after itself, promoting
restraint, forbidding folly and encouraging self-doubt. In
practice it can do quite the opposite. When aged eighteen,
following enthusiasm by others, I had chosen to go rock climbing, this apparently the thing to do. On the Idwal Slabs of
Snowdonia, as I still remember all too clearly, my booted toes
were resting on a 'ledge'. The others were using that little and
comforting word, although the protrusion was enabling only
one inch or so of boot to make uncertain use of it. There was
rope between me and the man above but that did not stop my
legs from gently shivering. And then shaking more determinedly. And finally, quite stupidly, causing that single boot of
mine to be distanced from the rock. Comforting words came
from up above, as that higher climber took the strain, but my
body had chosen to end its life by shaking me from the perch.
So much for loyalty. So much for taking care.

With every day that passed during our raft's construction I
had wondered why I was not abdicating from the project. Why
continue with the work (and the expense)? Why not truly comprehend the obstacle in front of us? And why not call myself
pigheaded as I had labelled that distant and departed friend?

8

I could potter, as others were advocating. I could watch little plants growing in their little yoghurt pots; so why jeopardize my life? I have no ready answer for such questioning. I only know the doubting part of me did not succeed and, in consequence, I had embarked upon the raft.

2

A very comforting fact arose that day of the rudder's failure. If something has broken there is probably much material then available to manufacture something else. Even if a plank has fractured centrally there are then two planks, each relatively short, but ready for a compromise. Our rudder had been a double affair, with two broad paddles joined by a structure that had held both sides in place. Apparently two crucial metal pins had snapped but only some of the paddle wood and none of the interlinking framework had fallen irretrievably into the sea. David, Andrew and John gathered all the remains, as I could plainly hear from my bunked position, before bringing them to the forward decking where there was more space. I could also listen to David giving orders, and realized that the breakage was not a disaster in his eyes but a kind of victory.

In the first place he had neither made the rudder nor had he advised about its style. In fact there had initially been discussion whether a rudder of any kind would be vital, the propensity of a raft to head nose-first being such an unknown quantity. Both the subsequent thinking and the creation had been performed by Tony Humphreys, the key member of the construction team who, back in Valle Gran Rey, had built more of the raft than anyone else. He had also been of considerable importance when visiting the Spanish maritime authorities. He let them have their say and thanked them for their help. His diplomatic tact was a vital ingredient in a very awkward business. No one had been in absolute charge of our raft's creation, an omission to be laid firmly at my door. I had seen no reason for a structured form of workforce and had hoped a kind of democracy would prevail, with everyone chipping in ideas as and when such thinking became important. The present task of making some jury-rig, with Tony back on land, was therefore up to sailing master David, and he, I think, was not totally displeased.

Another and quite different score was also settled, or at least adjusted, by the rudder break. I was financier of the venture because it was my enterprise. Sponsorship had helped by providing pipes and steel but my thinning wallet had bought the rest. No one was being paid to take part, either as crew or helpful friend, but I alone had to spend the money for most of the purchases made. My right hand had therefore been reaching for my back pocket most remorselessly. I tended to protest the moment I heard of some further alleged necessity but found it difficult to win each (or any) argument, being short of nautical experience to counter the numerous proposals. Did we really require a brand-new sea anchor; why not one second-hand or even no such thing? Why two GPS devices for detailing location when one was adequate? And why, causing disquiet to rise yet further, did we require additional means for generating electricity than the four costly solar panels already acquired and properly installed? Why a great big wind machine as well and why, for heaven's sake, a foot pedaller which created about as much power as a play wheel for a mouse might do?

'You can't compromise with safety,' said sailing-master David rather more than once, 'and a sound supply of electricity is a crucial safety feature.'

This sailing master really knew that compromise is possible, if not necessarily desirable in every circumstance. The individual signing cheques is bound to have a different opinion, and I certainly blew the famous gasket when three oars arrived one day costing a total of £750. Apparently I had given the nod for their purchase, not imagining for one moment such a price tag partnering mere oars. In consequence, following enlightenment, I could hardly speak. The longest one, admittedly a thing of well-made beauty, was priced at over £500. For one oar! For a raft!! For doing what??? Before departure, as we had put each of them onboard, the one of twenty-five feet – *TWENTY-FIVE FEET!* – and the two others each a mere fourteen feet in length, I thought that these unwelcome acquisitions might be sold profitably at some destination. Roll up, roll up, and buy untouched items of considerable beauty that have crossed the broad Atlantic!

But suddenly, and for a very reasonable £500, we had a potential steering sweep, likely to be as effective as any rudder once a wooden contrivance had been rigged with a suitably central hole through which this oar could go. After three days of hammering, screwing, sawing and nailing on our forward deck, the jury-rig announced its verdict: the new arrangement worked perfectly. The oar's immersion in the sea was easy to adjust, if moved sideways or up and down, with all such modest movements altering the actual direction in which we sailed. Best of all, unlike rudders needing near-perpetual attention, the exciting and novel contrivance worked splendidly entirely on its own.

'That sweep!' exulted David. 'It's so effective. Just a tweak alters our course almost immediately. Just a tiny little tweak. Quite astonishing!'

In short he had no problem with it, a favoured phrase of his. Andrew and John were also enthusiastic. They too did the tweaking when ordered to do so, and they each expressed amazement that such minor movements had such considerable effect. Neither of them ever disputed David's instructions (for he was the man in charge). They were both part-time sailors and therefore knew a thing or two, such as it not being their place to disagree. They were cabin boys, as John liked to describe himself, and it would be wrong for them – or anyone – to argue with the official master. That way lay error, particularly when urgency was important, and both these individuals understood this general dictum. I, lying down or sitting in my chair, liked what I saw and heard. The three of them, however recruited, were working as a team. All therefore seemed to be going well.

In many ways the trio looked similar. They were all of an age, with David fifty-seven, Andy fifty-six and John sixty-one. Not one was fat but neither was anyone skinny and their heights were more or less the same. David certainly spoke most and the other two were quieter, both apparently relaxed that the appointed sailing master had most to say, however far removed his chosen subject matter existed from the business of sailing and navigation. He liked telling tales from his past, often naming the girl who happened to be his partner at the time. If either of the other two told some story from their earlier days, David seemed duty-bound to match it, by telling of an incident in his memory which also involved customs officers, embarrassing head waiters, extreme thirst or mismatched clothing. He had certainly travelled widely and foreign stories are often thought to be better if hailing from Saudi Arabia, Gibraltar or deep within Tasmania. He never really spelled out his engineering work but neither did the other two of their jobs. I longed to hear lawyer John elaborate on the warfare he must have experienced, with couples or business partners hammering each other verbally and almost drawing blood. As for blood, I wanted lots of it from Doctor Andy. Surely patients had occasionally arrived at his surgery with a severed arm or mere fingers wrapped up in cloth? As for births he must have helped desperate women, perhaps in taxi cabs or deep within

Canadian snow, to deliver some brand-new and protesting human gasping for independence? I longed for secrets from the surgery, or the legal waiting room, or from some on-site workplace where a dodgy bit of engineering was being exposed, or fractured, or merely covered up, but – alas – I never heard such tales.

I personally like telling stories, and possibly told too many. I also like conversations that lead to some conclusion, with opinions surfacing and readjusted, and new facts revealed. After all, we four not only totalled two-and-a-half centuries in age but had experienced over 180 years of adulthood, working at our jobs, making errors, learning truths and gaining knowledge of some novel kind. We were not a bunch of youngsters, forever trampling on unfinished sentences, pretending wisdom of a worldly kind, laughing excessively as something to do and hoping to hold one's own. We were a team, working together, being punctual about watches, taking our turn at tasks, not hurting the others and knowing most assuredly that many weeks lay ahead of us during which no other humans would be encountered.

I found that to be the most disturbing realization on a very slow-moving raft. There would only be Dave and Andy and John for all the travelling days to come – these three and no others were my lot. Short of terrible misadventure our foursome was as fixed as the rising of the sun. I had, of course, always known that fact, but I knew it more intensely as those first days and nights passed by.

In the project's very earliest days I had also invited friends, and friends of friends, to come officially onboard, but no one had accepted. That had led to an advertisement in the *Daily Telegraph*: 'Wanted: three adventurous pensioners to sail by raft across the Atlantic'. I had also appeared on the *Richard and*

Judy Show, together with a model of the simple vessel I had hoped to recreate. About 150 applicants had subsequently got in touch, each giving thumbnail sketches of themselves.

'Served as Army cook for ten years.'

'My wife wants me to go.'

'Have GSOH.'

Unfortunately my eating of RAF meals for three-and-a-half years had formed unhappy prejudice against service food, along with its perpetrators. Even more did the great sense of humour (which those capitals indicate) cause all such individuals to be immediately discarded. Being told of steadfast merriment left me, I regret to say, very stony-faced. In any case I had somehow to whittle down the number. Even half a dozen arriving for interview occupied both time and management, with London's Euston Station as the chosen rendezvous. To everyone invited I gave a bun but I liked them all.

Only when one of them stood taller, after telling of his ability to 'speak Welsh and also write it', did I give him extra points. Of all the unbelievably fatuous assets, when rafting across Atlantic emptiness, there surely could not be one more likely to be useless, and I therefore underlined his name with extra fervour. Next to receive extra points that day was a St Albans man. He had allegedly once been hit on his head by a falling mast, another experience of doubtful value, and his birth had been in Tipperary. Places of arrival hardly explain a man but I suddenly foresaw one united kingdom of a very special kind. Already onboard was a Scot, a yachtsman six years my senior, whose only unhappy feature was an unending determination to tell Scottish jokes, these identical to Geordie/Cockney/Yorkshire jokes, save that those involved speak most incomprehensibly and hail, with every throaty syllable, from well to the north of the Tweed. I had certainly liked this international threesome. They were all affable and eager, with their ages definitely on the wrong side of sixty-five. Not one of them was letting this fact suppress his desire to carry on living much as he had already done.

I had hoped that this bun-rich, enthusiastic and elderly quartet would attract remuneration of some kind, but that age combination was our undoing, with me aged eighty-four and the Scotsman quite the worst of all. We would fail because we were old. It was that simple. There were no ifs or buts, and the uniquely united kingdom of individuals had had to be released.

Consequently I was suddenly left with a *Mary Celeste* of crewlessness. To advertise again, stressing that I wanted mature people still short of the pension watershed, seemed difficult. Therefore I chose to dither, with fortune, so they say, so often favouring the prepared mind. Into this vacuum, as luck would have it, the man named David Hildred walked into my flat one day. He explained that he was a fan. Worse than that, he apparently owned a copy of all my books, and quickly proved the point by knowing several of their stories better than I did. One such publication had been purchased by him, as a paperback priced 3/6d., when he was just thirteen. Apparently its tale of ballooning over Africa had inspired him to lead a travelling life, much as I had done. The little book (which had gained me three pence in royalties) had always voyaged with him and, as evidence, he produced the dog-eared thing, holding it reverentially as if some highly prized and early Gutenberg offering. On that initial meeting day he saw, and then gathered, all the VHS tapes I then owned of television films about various exploits in my past. He promptly took them to a photo shop where, at great expense (to him), they were transmuted into modern DVDs.

'Weird,' I thought.

'Was he weird in other ways?' asked worried friends on hearing of this individual.

It did not seem so. Aged fifty-seven, he had worked all his

life as a civil engineer, and had indeed laboured widely, from Saudi Arabia to Gibraltar, from Tasmania to bits of Africa. He had constructed his own boat, had often lived in it, and had frequently sailed it, mainly around the West Indies. Once he had been crew on a transatlantic yacht, and yachting was his favourite pastime. Various girlfriends had come and gone, much as girlfriends often do, but he was now married to a girl named Trish. Nothing too weird about any of that or about his place of residence, this being within the British Virgin Islands. Not many people live there but, with palm trees, warmth and general sunshine, the location was hardly weird. The more he spoke about himself the less I worried about his life-long admiration. Instead I realized that my *Celeste* might be about to become more occupied. And that was how it happened when I offered him the sailing reins.

'Could you possibly be the sailing master on this voyage that I'm now contemplating?'

There had been no hesitation before an affirmative reply came back, but this acceptance, although happily delivered and received, did have an important string attached. He would be grateful if a friend of his from mutual days at a primary school in Yorkshire could become another member of the team. Apparently these two had met at Harrogate and had stayed in touch during all the years since then. This similarly ancient buddy was also married, liked building things (such as his house), enjoyed sailing, was a GP, could take time off from work and lived in a fairly lonely part of Alberta, Canada. David offered to get in touch with this long-lasting companion, and I acquiesced. Two weeks later, and allegedly from a very snow-bound situation, Andrew Bainbridge MD was sending his acceptance. My *Celeste* was therefore not completely filled, in that Person No.4 still had to be acquired, but a quorum existed, a group able to exchange ideas about food and medicine, cookers and water storage, bunk size and all manner of rafting requisites. Sad Goodbyes had gone to the Scottish, Welsh and Irish individuals, these now replaced by big Hellos, both to the Virgin Islands and western Canada. It did seem odd for us to be so widely separated before we would become so intimately confined but, with emails and their like caring not a fig about proximity, there did not seem to be a problem.

Meanwhile I steadily asked good friends of mine to become the fourth individual and they equally steadily humbled me.

'My children will not let me go, the prospect being too dangerous.' (Mine were in favour of my departure, however hazardous.)

'I cannot leave one very sick friend.' (I too had sick friends but felt capable of leaving them.)

'It would be a selfish act to join you.' (So?)

'I could not leave the garden for that length of time.' (In winter?)

Days and weeks then ticked by and I still needed the important No.4. In my opinion four did seem a satisfactory number, good for watches, good for variety and good in general. I had also decided that no woman would be involved.

'They are a completely different sex,' to paraphrase Jack Lemmon when Marilyn M. first walked by in *Some Like It Hot*.

There is nothing wrong, of course, in that difference but a she onboard might upset the male apple cart quite dramatically. Whether three and one, or two and two, any pairing could cause rearrangements to happen and perhaps create pain. I thought that mere masculine togetherness might be sufficiently awkward without the extra ingredient of another kind, *the* other kind, of human being.

One evening this monastic structure had very nearly become unhinged. A gorgeous fifteen-year-old from Germany, with heavenly eyes peering coyly beneath an alluring fringe, offered to be our cook. Her nearby parents nodded at the suggestion while revealing that she had already sailed the ocean. This girl would undoubtedly contribute a different point of view about, well, almost everything and her age would, most properly, place her out of bounds. I took a sip of beer, thought of good meals, tried not to glance her way and sat looking at my knees before listening – as if from somewhere else – to what my throat was sadly saying.

'A lovely, lovely thought, but no.'

(Dearest Is, I cannot believe you have not landed on your feet since then, with great happiness all round.)

In the end, and following more time, it was David who suggested a possible number four, this man a solicitor, aged sixty-one, living near Oxford, and still working at Stroud in Gloucestershire where he had laboured at a desk for thirty-five years or so. He was married, as were David and Andrew, and another frequent sailor. I therefore despatched an invitation and his acceptance then came back almost before any message from me could possibly have arrived. The name of John Russell was therefore added to the list, but I would not be meeting him, any more than I would be meeting Andrew, before the two of them reached Valle Gran Rey, our construction base on La Gomera. Whether this tardiness mattered I had no idea. Until that time two of them would be blank slates, much like neighbouring strangers on trains or planes. Was such ignorance beneficial, with time having to pass before I became familiar with their oddities – and they with mine? Or was it stupid and foolhardy to be so ignorant, with mutual compatibility of great importance? Who knew such answers, for I did not. I only thought it peculiar that David knew all three of us, that Andrew knew David as did John, whereas I, the man allegedly in charge, knew least of all about the three of them. And two of them knew next to nothing about the man who had despatched their invitations.

* * *

Some ten days after our departure, the waves were becoming less ebullient and our course was shifting from south-west to nearer west. We were learning how to stay drier when outside the cabin door, and a certain routine was in place. I had ceased worrying about the Spanish authorities as we had journeyed more than 200 miles from their nearest land. The money problem had also become less disturbing. Apparently, according to Tony and Robin, crucial members of the construction team who had stayed behind to tidy up, the several kilometres of rope we had wrongly acquired (it had proved unnecessary when we had changed our minds about pipe binding and had chosen ratchet straps instead) had earned good cash to quieten most of the creditors into happy silence. I cannot praise either of this pair too highly. Tony was quite the busiest and Robin seemed to be doing just as much by running errands into town, buying most goods, these suddenly and urgently required, and certainly writing our expedition's blog, each day's diary of events, after we at sea had fed him with the necessary information. As for the chair which had casually been filched from our apartment, with my faulty legs needing something of the sort, its theft had been confessed to Señora Carmen, owner of that dwelling plus much else. She had apparently expressed delight at her contribution to our epic and would have done the same, so she had said, for Cristóbal Colón when he too set sail, and he would doubtless have been as pleased.

By now on the journey David had become Dave, Andrew from Canada was Andy, and John was John. I had also learned more of each man's marital status. Dave, for all his partnerships, had only married once and to the girl named Trish. Andy had married twice, with Beryl – his second wife – accompanied by her two grown children (whereas Andy had no children of his own). John had also been married twice, the first ending in divorce when their three children had reached adulthood, and the second – to Sue, who was accompanied by a child. Strangely, this new wife of his had also known David in their earlier years. I, to complete this complex picture of further liaisons, had been married twice, divorced twice and fathered three children. Between us, we four had experienced a total of seven marriages, these linked to three step-children and six of the traditional variety. The record was hardly perfect but these are modern times.

My three onboard crew, whatever their situations back home, were each kind to the project's instigator. They chose to let me off certain tasks because, gibbon-like, I needed handholds even when standing upright and certainly when moving about the place. Helpful sticks were useless against the raft's perpetual and uneven rocking. Instead, numerous and handy anchor points had been fashioned mainly out of fabric, and these were much used by me in particular. Even so, a good many tasks still proved too difficult, such as cooking, opening tins or helping with the sail. Try stirring edibles on the cooker with one hand and little will happen save for a spinning pan. Do not even think of using a corkscrew or cutting anything when only one arm is available (and assuredly resent all those yachts which, allegedly, are sailed *single-handedly* around the world – such an exploit would get a loud huzzah from me).

The crew, not to be outdone by my consequent laziness, quickly thought up other tasks which could be performed by anyone sitting down, such as washing up, peeling potatoes or slicing bread. No one bettered me in the slicing business, partly because no one else ever even tried. We thought bread-baking to be a most civilized activity for our ocean voyage, and the means were all available – one oven, bags of flour, sufficient yeast and loads of time; but it has to be said, particularly by the one who never baked, that there must have been something faulty in this bread-creating business. On day one after baking, although a lovely smell was redolent, the actual product crumbled pathetically at the mere approach of a saw-edged knife. By day two, having had twenty-four hours to think things over, it had hardened into very much sterner stuff. Our blades were, no doubt, at the cutting edge of knife technology, but they caused me to remember Italian marble quarries where travertine, for example, is severed by circulating wire-rope for days and days on end. I know what I am talking about with our thrice-weekly loaves because I alone performed the task of carving them. If rock-hard bread planks were wanted I would furnish them, and therefore set aside an hour or so per loaf to perform this all-important work.

3

Long before rafts, reefs or Bahamas had become important, or even relevant, I had contemplated crossing the Atlantic – somehow. Back in 1942, when in a different epoch of my life, I had already learned of the ocean's equatorial current that travels from east to west, this obligingly serving as transport medium from the Old World to the New. I did not see it as a form of escalator (as it is often described) because at that time I had never seen such things, but more as one colossal river, something akin to Tom Sawyer's Mississippi, as the home in which I then lived lay very near the Thames. Then to that comfortable world of childhood, happily distanced during World War Two from all the bombing, my father had brought home a book one day called *Two Survived*. It told of a Merchant Navy ship's sinking not far from the Canary Islands which had led to seven men clambering into the only undamaged lifeboat. These sailors, knowing a thing or two, then headed west and not to those islands lying a few hundred miles to the east of them. Without an engine and with only a diminutive sail, there was no way they could have reached that nearest land because both wind and current would have been against them. Instead, and in the opposite direction, they were confronted by 2,700 miles of ocean travel before reaching somewhere like the Leeward Islands on the Atlantic's other side. As it happened, and after seventy days, their little boat had arrived at the Bahamas which lie further to the north. And, as it also happened, creating the most terrifying portion of this awesome tale, only two of the seven men were still alive when land was there to greet them after a desperate ten weeks. The other seamen had mainly died by abandoning their little craft, stepping over its side and preferring death at sea to the extreme pain caused by entrails starved so lengthily, both of water and of food.

As a boy I had relished the war until that time. A like-minded chum had earlier written of 'not being bombed yet, worse luck'. Neither had I, but I had totally enjoyed watching distant London being attacked, considering the sudden bursts of fire better than anything ever seen on Guy Fawkes' evenings. On one occasion the next-door field had been showered with incendiaries, these jettisoned from a German bomber, its crew no doubt desperate to lose weight and gain some speed. I had rushed around, gasping gratitude to the vanished plane and heaping extinguishing earth upon the spluttering things before bringing them home to rest, half-consumed and still most flammable, upon our mantelpiece. As for poison gas, I had welcomed the wholesale distribution of masks to keep us safer (truly, and for how long?) merrily, and without trepidation, partly because splendid farting noises were possible when expelling rather than welcoming gasps of air. The war, in short, was fun. At school we dug trenches in zigzag fashion, and there were fewer masters for all the forms. Days off work were numerous and we lifted potatoes, destroyed hedgerows (thus making bigger fields), smashed saucepans for their aluminium, removed lead from churches, their brass from elbow rests on pews, and took everything we could 'for the war'. There is nothing quite like destruction to please small boys, with permitted – and patriotic – devastation making it better still. What luck it was that silly old uni-testicular

Hitler, as we sang when given an ounce of opportunity, had so disrupted the school routine. What fun it was to have a war – but then, in 1942, and aged sixteen, I read that book.

It was the suicides that so appalled me. I did not dwell on the thirty-four men who had been killed and drowned in that ship's sinking, or on the twenty-year-old radio operator who had swiftly died from gangrene (as one of his feet was smashed), but I absolutely focussed on the Royal Marine, he being the only gunner onboard the lifeboat and swiftest to abdicate. Next was the First Officer who, together with an engineer, quietly discussed the matter before taking off their shirts, removing their rings (for safe keeping by others who might survive) and relishing deep draughts of sea water before stepping into all that sea. Neither man had then lifted his head. They each did nothing, save drift arm in arm until no longer visible. These two, plus the Marine, had preferred to live no more, considering death the better option. So this was a side-effect of war! And it was war which later killed the junior cook onboard, with him allegedly 'going mad' before walking the boat's length, mumbling inanely about 'heading for the pub', tumbling into the ocean, and also making no attempt to lift his head or swim. The two youngsters still remaining, aged nineteen and twenty-one, did both try to end their lives but swam around instead before climbing back onboard, and just sleeping, losing half their body weight and eventually grounding on the bright white-pink sand bordering the Bahamian island of Eleuthera. As a final horror to this tale, the slightly older (and married) man was first to recover, and was therefore first to be shipped back home. U-69 saw the converted liner transporting him when that ship was one day out from Liverpool and sank it speedily, thus drowning everyone onboard.

In later years, having learned a little biology, it also appalled me that nothing like a fish hook was ever installed within a lifeboat. In consequence men were dying dreadfully when floating on the bonanza of a massive sea. So why not catch fish? If one is squeezed, so I had discovered, the delivered juice is drinkable. Its taste may be unpleasant but the gathered liquid can help to keep a man alive, along with the flesh itself. Provisions were often stolen from lifeboats, providing extra food for rationed families back home, but hooks and lines and lures would surely have stayed onboard, thereby keeping men alive in such boats rather than encouraging them to step over-board and wretchedly end their days.

Of course, like several million others, I read about the Kon-Tiki Expedition of 1947. The six on board plainly had a great time, catching fish (including sharks) and proving the efficiency of rafts. They did not aim for any particular island but the six Scandinavians had undoubtedly served as inspiration. Neither food nor anything else appeared to be a problem.

It was in 1952, when I had finished with both service life and university, that three of us planned – somehow – to test the bounty of the sea and drift, with wind and current as sole assistants, across some major bit of sea. We therefore bought, for extremely modest price, a small Belgian boat entirely short of engine or of mast or sails. In fact, we were busily planning our Atlantic crossing on this craft when a Frenchman named Alain Bombard pipped us to the post. In a rubber dinghy, and with a food supply securely locked, he reached the ocean's other side after consuming only what the sea had given him. We promptly realized that our exploit would be seen as second fiddle to his courageous enterprise. In any case our entire and united capital – some £300 – had by then become exhausted, and we three soon dispersed to go our separate ways. I do not know if the others still lingered for a crossing, but do know that such a possibility then never died in me.

Far from dying or being forgotten, the desire actually increased as the many years passed by. Like some first love never being toppled from its supremacy, the Atlantic wish remained intact. I had no such feelings about the Pacific or any other mass of water, just as second loves can never overtake the first. There was also no wish to travel from east to west on anything other than a raft. This form of travel, so superior in my mind to a boat, was enmeshed with the Atlantic, with each both part and parcel of the old desire. I did once cross that ocean on a three-masted square rigger, voyaging (for modest price) from Bermuda to Southampton, but this journey was – quite wrongly – from west to east and therefore did nothing to subdue the ancient longing. I took no interest in charts showing other major currents around the world, but never forgot the North Atlantic impetus that had transported those two sailors from the region of their sinking to their island of salvation. People often have alleged desires – opening a café on Tahiti, taking a dog sled for weeks on end, travelling by bus to Timbuktu – but never achieve such wishes as they are a form of make-believe. With me I *had* to cross the Atlantic, just as I *had* to go by raft. There was no logic to this longing; it was just a part of me. If I were to reach my deathbed without any such fulfilment I would hate such a wrongful ending, both deeply and quite miserably. The crossing merely had to be achieved. Other people have other addictions which they cannot vanquish. I too could not dismember the ancient longing; it simply had to come to pass.

Worse still, for friends to comprehend when hearing of my plans, I wished to re-enact the journey taken by those two young sailors, in so far as this was possible. They had landed on the island of Eleuthera; I therefore wished to follow suit. They had grounded upon a particular beach and I would try to match, most precisely, that actual ending place, however impossible this might prove to be. It is always good to have a destination, even on a stroll through a piece of countryside. Consequently my desire to re-enact their voyage hardened as the years passed by, and certainly when the trip became increasingly feasible. I could hardly start where their vessel had been sunk, and I saw no reason for starvation of the kind those sailors had experienced, but I would disregard, if possible, all the other West Indian islands and concentrate upon the Bahamas. I would then head for that group's easternmost piece of land, namely the narrow strip that is called Eleuthera. And finally, while I was about it, I might as well aim for the self-same beach that the men had reached. Why choose anywhere else? Why not follow them exactly? The raft might end up going to another place, like some wayward arrow meeting a target's outer rim, but an archer aims for the central bull and I would do the same.

Therefore fast-forward, as they say, to 2005, when I was holidaying on the Canary Islands and, more specifically, on the one named La Gomera. This extraordinary piece of land, only recently created (as geologists use that term), possessed the small town of Valle Gran Rey on its western side. This compressed settlement enchanted me and I strode about its narrow streets most happily, particularly at their southern end where a little harbour was as secure and handsome an anchorage as could possibly be desired. There were apparently plans to make it bigger, to receive car ferries as well as people carriers, and some dead ground had been cordoned off while waiting to be excavated. Suddenly, as if with a trumpet's clarion call, I realized I was looking at a prime construction site for the building of a raft. The area was off-limits to normal individuals. Security staff patrolled it, and the attractive town – with an immediate assortment of cafés, shops, apartments and restaurants – was extremely close at hand. What was therefore stopping me from starting work at once? Nothing, save that I had no sponsorship, no fellow dreamers and certainly no money of the quantity that would be necessary.

I then met Brian Smith, an old ballooning acquaintance. He

was an Australian visiting London and I happened to mention rafts (as indeed had become a tedious tendency). He listened quietly while I rambled and he behaved like many another soul inflicted with my talk, save that – and on the morrow – he had constructed four identical little rafts. These were rect-angular and each equipped with a cardboard sail.

'Let's go to Kensington Round Pond,' he said, 'as I want to test a theory.'

Plainly this Brian was in quite a different category to others who had listened; in fact he is in a different category to every-one else I know. Anyway, no sooner said than done and, equipped with his four raft-lets, we were soon brushing aside small boys playing enthusiastically and noisily with hopelessly waterlogged craft or even with vessels actually upside down, as we committed our far more important creations to that pre-cious slab of water. Brian wanted to know if lengths of string attached, either port or starboard, to their sterns would guide them differently across the pond. Indeed this is precisely what they did. Left-side string took them to the left and starboard string contrarily.

'So?' said one small boy, master of a craft dripping generously in his arms.

'So we can steer without a rudder,' Brian replied, thus answering both me and the hugely sodden one as well.

Thus it happened, as things can do, that he invited me to Melbourne. And thus it also happened that, before too long, he was meeting me at his local airport and driving us to his home. Many a youngster likes a garden shed where he can do all manner of things – make bangs, mix chemicals outrage-ously and keep clear of parents – but Brian has taken this custom to new heights by turning a shed into a home. This dwelling is almost a hundred feet long and some thirty feet wide, in fact quite big enough to install a mobile ten-ton crane. Somewhat inevitably there is one, along with one (or more) of every other kind of item that exists – a mannequin, all the tools of every trade, bits and pieces of balloons, further bits and pieces of earlier enthusiasms, and objects with no remembered provenance. As the man said when peering for the first time into Tutankhamun's tomb and urgently asked for information: 'I see things, beautiful things.' Perhaps Brian's things are not quite as beautiful but each has had its day when prime object of some all-consuming activity pulsing through his brain. And there is also Chrissie who has created a very feminine quarter to one side of the bedlam that is so dominant.

'I think we should make Mark 1 out of water pipes,' said Brian, well ahead of me as ever.

And that is what we did. Chrissie fed us from time to time, often with exquisite mangoes, while he and I hammered, screwed, lifted, fixed, glued, planed and did whatever seemed crucial at the time. Fortunately the city of Melbourne, and particularly its industrial area, possesses skips in abundance and these we often visited for their advantages. In particular there were bits of water pipe and these we treasured because they would form a substrate (following various purchases) for Mark 1. If bound together, both horizontally and crosswise, we would have the makings of a raft. And, within a commendably short time, that is what we placed on wheels before towing it to a side-arm of Port Philip Bay, this normally home to pelicans and the very occasional human fishermen. It had been a relief to leave the two lanes of the major highway that we had fully occupied and then an even greater relief when our construction proved that it floated perfectly in between all those birds, each as oddly shaped for flight as our vessel was for travelling at sea.

Brian had learned that ancient Peruvians had used a mesh of 'guaras' for their rafts before the Spanish arrived to dismiss such navigational aids, along with the craft that they apparently assisted. (Colonists tend to dismiss the local expertise that they encounter as being primitive or plain wrong.) Basically a guara is a kind of plank that can be raised or lowered from its protrusion beneath the raft. It is not a keel but a sort of dagger-board or lee-board that amends the vessel's heading. What is difficult to assess, as Brian had also learned from books, is the actual change to be expected when each guara is deployed. Basically it is a suck-it-and-see system, with wind direction, current direction, the desired course and actual course all relevant to the mix. We therefore, pelicans permitting, wished to experiment with the seven guaras we had created.

And that, once again, is what we did. Our first amazement was the speed at which Mark 1 altered its course when we changed a guara's depth – it was as good as instantaneous and we were overjoyed. I personally also liked just standing on our raft, it being some twenty feet long and ten feet wide. There was a mast, this equipped with a modest sail, and it helped to keep me upright as we manoeuvred our way between buoys, position markers and other upright things in that locality. I therefore thought of other localities, such as the Atlantic, and wondered what it might feel like to be confronted by nothing but thousands of miles of nothingness save sea. In short I longed to be off, save of course for a few incidentals still in the way – such as a crew and cash and many more pipes and a cabin and a mast and whatever else stood between a dream and the real world which tends to obtrude so massively, however much we may wish to let it go.

'Chicken or not-chicken?' I think she said as I settled into my seat for the long haul back home.

'Any mangoes?' I asked, but answer came there none.

Now that I was away from Brian, from Chrissie, my bedside mannequin, the pelicans and Mark 1, I began to realize that a considerable lack still existed in the matter of my wishing to

cross the Atlantic by ocean-going raft. For example, funding
had shrunk as one consequence of Melbourne. There was still
at that time no crew to keep me company, nor were pipes
ready and waiting for burglary from skips or even purchases
from shops. It was sad about the mangoes but sadder still
about all the other deficiencies, these keeping me company as
I and 400 others travelled from one side of the planet to
another. My mood also shifted by 180 degrees as the journey
took me from happy optimism to stark reality. How on earth,
and when on earth, could things improve?

Fortunately – if that is the word – I then experienced an
extremely damaging accident. A van's driver, reversing both
blindly and much too speedily upon a piece of pavement, was
plainly at fault and I was certainly the victim. Before losing
consciousness I knew that I was underneath that van's rear
axle, having cleverly dodged its differential. Cleverness was
also paramount with my memory of the vehicle's registration
number. I did not realize that the ambulance team had been
snipping off my clothes from top to bottom, the better to discover what other injuries might have been incurred, but I
proudly told that van's number to a disbelieving constable. He
did have cause for doubt, as I was making little sense in
general, but I had been maddened by the driver's abrupt
disappearance (having pulled me from beneath), with him
neither contacting 999 nor staying on the spot.

Someone else, a passer-by and much later, then dialled for
help, and my memory was proved correct after the police had
knocked upon the door where that Luton-type van had been
registered. I then asked, during a coherent moment, if clever
work with DNA would match the accident to that vehicle, with
some of my blood assuredly involved. The attendant policeman by my hospital bed even laughed most merrily when
providing an answer to this questioning.

'Oh no, Sir, no need for that. You see, there were bits and pieces of your eyebrow on his rear axle.'

The mishap caused me to spend thirty-nine days in hospital. Its staff replaced much of one femur with metal before stitching certain portions of my damaged face and helping me walk again – although much less properly than before. I do not adore hospitals in general but do welcome the desire to care that is so prevalent among most of those labouring within their walls. It must be tedious attending to patients who cannot be bothered to visit any of the toilets before achieving self-relief or others who wail, particularly loudly every night, but nurses are ludicrously kind about each inmate's petty triumphs.

'Oh well done, Anthony,' they say, after some minor brilliance has been achieved, like getting out of bed, swallowing a pill or remembering a nurse's name.

I can take any amount of such worship, morning, noon and – particularly – during the smallest hours of night. Less fun are all the carers who surface after patients are taken home again.

'I see your smoke alarm isn't working.'

'Can you make it work?'

'No, I'm not an electrician.'

'Are you an electrician?'

'Yes, but I can't reach it.'

'Well, stand on this stool and I'll hold you.'

'What! Held up by a cripple! I'd be a laughing stock.'

The physiotherapists within hospitals are in a very different league. They seem to be aged twenty, beautifully packaged inside crisp and spotless uniforms, and care not at all that many of their clientele are *four times* their age. Such as the woman of ninety-five who shared my ward's corridor. She always ordered shepherd's pie for lunch and then, like some slender reed gradually shorn of strength, lowered her face directly into it. After she had been rescued, and generally cleaned, she, I and others were once taken 'for a spot of physio'. This entailed throwing beach balls at each other. The elderly lady never caught one of them, or even seemed to notice that these inflated things, so unlike pies of any kind, were actually landing near her silent situation. Eventually the whiter-than-white therapists muttered to each other, removed a card from a cabinet and suggested that we should elect a 'Man of the Match'. What an absurd idea! Such a title had no place in a room to which at least a thousand years of living had been carefully wheelchaired; but, with much winking from the staff, a few of us began to understand that the ninety-fiver should be our choice. Therefore those patients who could do so promptly raised their arms. Indeed her name was already on the card. That was given to her, almost formally, but nothing happened for quite a while. Then, to the relief and joy of everyone, an exquisite smile broke forth. This was totally ravishing and absolutely radiant – it was supreme. As I say, the desire to care does lie at the base of hospital staff, whether at physio, at mealtimes, at long-distance wheelchairing or even during the noisiest hours of night.

In between the accident and my picking up the threads of normal life again, the all-important matter of compensation had arisen. There were those extremely jolly and reassuring people on television who excitedly tell of 'No Win, No Fee'. Surely I could gain some cash because, also surely, I was the innocent party?

'It's open and shut,' a policeman had said, 'if you ask me.'

I had not asked but it did seem sensible to enquire. There may be care at the base of hospitals, but there is certainly greed and appetite near the base of every individual. Money would not go amiss, we say. We could even give it away, we lie. Anyway, I soon phoned a recommended number, and a man was knocking on my door one day later. He took notes, extensively. We visited 'the scene of the crime' some fifty yards from my front door. The man heard – at length – about my operation, this being on Christmas Eve no less, and he saw my reliance upon two sticks.

'Yup, open and shut, if you ask me.'

Once again I had not asked, but the man was well ahead of me.

'There are only two things I can't tell you,' he added before departing. 'That's how much you'll get and when.'

These, basically, were the only questions buzzing through my head. Of course I asked for clues, but none was given: I would simply have to wait and see. Therefore I did wait and I did, eventually, see. The time between claim and payment proved to be a year and a half but the figure on the cheque was twice as much as even my optimism had expected.

No wonder that the raft idea had then suddenly leaped forward. I called this compensation windfall a form of seed money and started to spend the manna that had arrived, not so much from heaven but from an office block in Leeds. My dream of crossing the Atlantic, east to west, by raft, might finally come to pass.

4

After two weeks upon the raft a routine had definitely been established. I thought it amazing that we could each be so matter of fact about our novel situation, brushing our teeth in standard fashion, washing clothes and hanging them to dry as if always onboard a flat and bouncing thing buoyed up by lots of pipes.

All of our eighteen polyethylene tubes had been donated by a kindly company based at Huntingdon, namely the four fat ones forming the base and fourteen smaller crosswise lengths in which all of our drinking water was contained. We were therefore a form of quadmaran with extreme buoyancy at our command, our twelve-ton total weight causing only a foot or so of draught between the sea's surface and the deepest bit of pipe. The cabin was made of corrugated steel, this being the material beneath which single sows are often housed these days to keep their numerous piglet progeny from being damagingly trampled by alien porcine feet. Known as pig arks, such dwellings now speckle much of the British countryside and, as the corrugated steel was donated, also served for us.

With pipes and steel forming such a major part of the raft's construction it might seem as if expense had effectively been sidelined, but not a bit of it. We'd acquired a telegraph pole to serve as mast, and another to act as spar enabling our thirty-six square metres of sail to be raised and angled as need be. British law does permit bath tubs to go to sea, once properly registered, but the world of electronics cannot now be disregarded. Initials, such as GPS, AIS and EPIRB, well known to every sailor, let the world know, and all sailors know, not only where they currently exist but who else is in the vicinity and precisely where some mishap has occurred should a sinking or other gross misfortune ever come to pass.

Yachts have been likened to demanding monsters in the backyard, forever consuming and perpetually hungry. Rafts differ not one jot. There is always something more to buy – lights, a cooker, fuel, pots, pans, bedding, storage boxes, a toilet (or two), flags, a dinghy, a life-raft (with attendant grab bag), ratlines, aerials, storage bins, cleats, netting, laptops, torches, field glasses, twelve-volt batteries, an electrical regulator, compass, camera gear, charts and even notebooks in which to write down such lists. All I ask for is a tall ship, a star to steer her by and better charts, four vacuum mugs, several non-slip coasters, more flares, spare batteries and, oh yes, some cheap tin trays. The monster's appetite is never fully assuaged. Ask any yacht owners what is still desirable and their answers will surface without delay. Ask any rafter and he is just the same. It is like wondering what a whole house still needs. Of course there is more that could, or might, or probably, would be useful. And everything has to fit, as with furnishing a home, within the confinements still available.

Now we were on our way, I longed to see us with everything onboard. What did we look like on the forty by eighteen feet contrivance that formed our home? Once, when with my motor bicycle in a very lonely part of Africa, I had heaved the machine on to its stand, left the engine running and walked away from it, the better to appreciate both the sight and sound that it and I were making when journeying through such a hugely empty land. The noise stayed astonishingly audible, seemingly for ever. So did the bike's metallic brightness stay visible as I steadily increased the growing distance between it and me. Eventually I saw a car, identified initially solely by its accompanying column of dust, coming along that road. After reaching my machine two men got out of their own vehicle, walked briefly, looked around and failed to see me waving while jumping distantly up and down, much like a flea upon the back of an elephant. They then switched off my engine before speeding northwards yet again. That was a bad move, as the bike was always difficult to start when hot, but the lengthy walk had given me insight into my ludicrously minuscule status in the broad scheme of things.

So too, I imagined, with the raft. It was surely as nothing within the great Atlantic, and yet we onboard were carrying on as if it were a standard day and a standard situation. We were the only people for hundreds of miles on either side of us, and yet were hanging up washed items as if normality was in charge. I shivered a little at the thoughts then buzzing through my head.

'Talk about odd!' I said out loud, and was immediately grateful that no one else had heard. Andy was softly learning another chord on his guitar, John crouched to read and Dave untying some tangle involving what he always named as string.

What were these three thinking about their extreme form of isolation? Might one of them be on some knife edge, about to snap when total realization gained control, when the fact of no more people truly made its mark? I had once been in a lift that had come to a sudden halt. Of course we onboard had promptly used the available telephone and informed the outside world of our situation. We learned that our state was likely to last awhile, before some helpful mechanic could arrive with the necessary tools and expertise. That did not stop one of our number attempting to telephone again (and again), to repeat the facts already given, to suggest more haste, to be a most unwelcome member of our little group. We very nearly came to blows within that space, with nerves jangling and hatred gaining force. I suppose we suffered in that container for thirty minutes and I know we each loathed every one of them. On our raft there were many weeks ahead of us, or probably a couple of months, and no form of helpful mechanic was on the horizon whichever way we looked.

In the early days, and before starting on construction, we had officially – and properly – registered *Antiki*, this name partly to bow humbly before the great *Kon-Tiki* of 1947 and also to admit that the crew's senior status and longevity were not irrelevant. (We had to omit a hyphen because registration law these days forbids any such inclusion.) I was sad that the great Thor Heyerdahl had never learned of our adulation for his raft journey across the Pacific Ocean, as he and his crew had all vanished by the time of our venture. I was particularly and personally mortified because I had known the man. We had shared the same publisher in London and I certainly remembered the considerable in-house, pre-publication argument about a suitable title for his most famous book. Was *The Kon-Tiki Expedition* too much of a mouthful, too difficult to say and even to memorize?

Plainly it was not, because, shortly after the decision had been made and publication day had arrived, the corridors, stairways and meeting rooms of 40 Museum Street, WC1, were stacked almost to the ceiling with packets of his work. Three printing companies were doing nothing else than creating yet more packages of this phenomenal bestseller. As an aspiring author I was most impressed. What riches could come one's way via lovely royalties! What a future lay in store, what wealth and also – for it might as well be said – what considerable disappointment if one's own pathetic sales did not match (to any degree) those for the adventurous Norwegian.

I certainly met Thor at his Colla Micheri home near

Laigueglia, nearish to the coastline north of Italy's Genoa. There he told how he had persuaded the local authorities to put a preservation order on the landscape's beauty where his home existed, but he then had need – following another marriage – to extend his dwelling. Other officials from the local comune quickly explained to him that nothing could be changed because 'some extremely recent legislation had forbidden any such alteration'. We laughed, of course, and also spoke of reed boats, of Easter Island, archaeology in the Canaries, Lake Titicaca, wartime Norway, his children and heaven knows what else, such as his running naked from a hotel in Managua during the earthquake of 1972 and then rushing back, with the building teetering and many rooms squashed flat, for his passport and some clothes. But we never spoke about rafts, how they travelled, and what he had learned during those extraordinary days – 101 in all – which had so captivated so many millions around the world.

In particular, and before our voyage, I had wanted to know what it felt like when travelling on a raft. How upsetting, for mood and for potentially mobile objects, would be the steady rocking, and how tiring would it be, even at night, when securely bunked to gain some rest? After two weeks we ourselves knew many of the answers. There was undoubtedly the steady back and forth but this had more effect on people, particularly those with stupid legs, than on bottles, mugs, jars or indeed anything which might be longing for a spell of liberty. To our astonishment – and certainly to the three sailors of the crew – nothing on our raft ever spilled or toppled. I had spent chunks of time on small yachts, where everything on tabletops had so frequently preferred to leap somewhere else. On our raft even the top-heavy and bottled condiments bought for *Antiki* were quite content to stay where we had placed them. Books on shelves had no need of little battens to keep them secure and they could also be piled sideways without ever tumbling to a lower level. Yes, the raft did go up and down, laterally, longitudinally and without a single pause, but there was never need for us to grovel on hands and knees when hoping to retrieve, say, the HP sauce, after it had fallen and gurgled out its contents far from its original situation.

Dave, who often chose a dissimilar path to others and who had spent the greatest time afloat, accepted this fact with gratitude and never seemed to query it. Andy may have queried it internally, but he expressed no opinion out loud, as was his distinctive way. John was also content to let the matter ride and rested his coffee mug near him on the deck, knowing it would stay that way however rough the sea. I longed for more talk, and opinion, and chat from the three of them, and then wondered if that was a better option than longing for reduction. On reflection, quite probably it was, but there were many more weeks to go.

At that two-week stage, and rather more importantly, I worried less about the raft's construction than previously. Dave was different. He did not seem to care that amateurs (such as the four of us) had made most of the decisions, with sub-amateurs (such as our numerous assistants) doing a great deal of the work. He 'had no problem with that'. Instead he emphasized that each pipe, even if full of water and becoming independent, would still float and we should take comfort from that fact. For me the thought was only modestly pleasing – how on earth could we rest on, and stay attached to, smooth and slippery cylinders, however buoyant they might be? John, in practical fashion, merely assumed death should the raft turn upside down. I do not know what Andy thought; on this subject, he never voiced opinion.

As for pipes in general, I had long-since favoured them over wooden logs, even if such timber was light like balsa, ever since

Brian had filched a portion of pipe from his nearest skip for our prototypes, encouraging him to buy some more. With this inspirational example I had arrogantly approached GP Systems at Huntingdon and they had showed off not only their factory but half of a nearby airfield stacked with piles of pipes awaiting delivery, these coloured blue, yellow or black for their eventual purposes (of transporting water, gas or sewage). This organization had promptly sympathized with my request for pipe donation but then had further thoughts. There was, of course, no wish – by anyone – that GP Systems might be in any way to blame should some mishap come our way. The skip sample, which I'd brought back from Australia, was soon and determinedly dismissed by them as too light, too thin and much too breakable. In its place our benefactors had suggested that the four big pipes should have walls sufficiently thick to withstand any amount of battering against reefs or rocks that might come their way. This formidable pipe four-some, each with a two-foot diameter, would create the raft's lower level, and every such pipe would have its open ends securely capped, with GP Systems arranging for the capping. This was all very well, and most generous, but the change caused my happy-go-lucky Tom Sawyer thinking to fly from the window. It meant that each of the major pipes would now weigh 1.25 tons, thus making five tons in all. The fourteen others, a mere twelve inches in diameter, would each be a great deal lighter but their number would assuredly add more tonnage to the total. Tom, Huck and Joe, you happily lived in quite a different world (of Mark Twain's imaginings) and not in the twenty-first century within which I was now solidly – and expensively – involved.

In short, I was forced to accept the notion, and the costly hiring, of a forty-foot container, largest of the considerable breed within which much modern merchandise is now transported by road and sea from place to place. At Huntingdon one such thing duly arrived for us to fill – with every object we required for the raft to partner all those pipes of polyethylene, such as 640 square feet of wooden planking (to serve as deck), two telegraph poles for mast and spar, one square sail, four sizeable solar panels plus two large batteries to maintain their electrical generation, a panel of electronic gear to consume much of it, some twenty-five two-foot boxes filled to the brim with food, timber to be fashioned into saddles between both kinds of pipe, corrugated steel to make our single dwelling and countless extras which helped to fill the huge container that we had – so expensively – acquired. Despite this thing's considerable length, and its eight-foot width plus eight-foot height, we almost filled its 2,560 cubic feet of internal space. I was impressed, but also somewhat deflated by the huge assembly of necessary things. Practically all of it had been paid for – by me. The cornucopia of compensation cash, that seed money which had so accidentally arrived, had by now been vanished absolutely, and so had a great deal more. Of course the seed had grown, had needed extra nourishment, and I had steadily groaned when confronted by each new 'necessity' before it was added to the pile. Nevertheless, Tony, Robin and I all patted that container fondly after nearly filling it at Huntingdon.

'What about a kettle?' someone said.

'Here's a kettle,' said someone else, almost immediately.

'And a bicycle,' said someone else, with a spare one in his car.

'And a traffic cone; could be useful.'

'And some ancient clothes.'

And I forget what else because it was that kind of day. We hoped to see all these possessions again, provided that Felixstowe's extraordinary container-dock did its job correctly and delivered the items as need be in approximately ten days' time. The forty-foot and bright-red thing created in Hamburg was then scheduled to reach Valle Gran Rey and, to our happy and relieved astonishment, it arrived punctually on the promised date. After forcing open its impressively heavy doors at the construction site we not only greeted its piled-high contents with many a heartfelt pat, but were delighted to congratulate the donated kettle still resting on top of everything precisely where we had placed it. In short, this was one magnificent occasion and Tony, Robin, the recently arrived David Hildred and I immediately celebrated at the Café Puerto, each of us extremely conscious of the quantity of assembly which lay ahead. The arrival date (at VGR as we quickly named the place) was 22 November and I had earlier written that 3 January 2011 should witness fulfilment of our labour, after considering that some sort of deadline would be helpful. That meant a mere six weeks to build something which none of us had ever built before, a craft good enough to sail the entire Atlantic and also sufficiently manageable to navigate rather than travel straight downwind. We were not a yacht but, on the other hand, we had no wish to be a piece of flotsam without control. In fact, we had every intention of proving that rafts can have definite destinations, not quite everywhere but certainly well to the right or left of straight downwind.

We four onboard *Antiki* were subsequently amazed that we had put the raft together, with it doing so well – rudder apart – and then found it easy to forget the wide range of people who had been so crucial. We had not been ready by 3 January because rain, Christmas, New Year, Twelfth Night and formidable gales had all got in the way, but without our volunteers the construction time would have been a great deal longer. These extra individuals were mainly passers-by who had stopped and stared too lengthily, encouraging us to suggest they might wish to hammer something, tie a knot or lift the other end of heavy planking.

A man named Nicasio extracted our massive and lengthy pipes from the container before placing them on the ground – and to the nearest inch – where we had wanted them. Neither our Tony nor he could speak each other's languages, or even attempt to do so, but that definite lack had proved to be no problem. Tony had gesticulated, much as conductors do with orchestras, and had raised his arms, lowered them, pointed a finger or simply beckoned until the unloading job was done. Nicasio's mammoth machine, gushing black smoke when obeying its master's orders, had eventually been swivelled backwards on its gigantic wheels before vanishing to town with its very contented driver bouncing at the wheel.

By this same method we had acquired Hardy, a German with a much admired 1930s' bicycle, along with a certain bankrupt carpenter, as he himself proclaimed. Then there were Carine and Lisa, delectable themselves but, better still, generally arriving with exquisite chocolate. A local man named Steve also arrived who, as with every other resident ex-pat, told of the £400 heating allowance annually received – in the Canaries! – from British pension welfare. A slim Romanian girl wore hardly a conventional stitch, although her tattoo made her seemingly fully dressed. Adam and Rotem, both from Israel who, quite disregarding Health and Safety, strolled barefoot without care from pipe to pipe. There were also several German families unaware of the elation – *gehobene Stimmung* – given when telling that a little word like zip was *Reissverschluss* in their tongue. There was one dotty Dane with Lycra shorts, and an infinitely greater Dane named Aelfred who came by near-horizontal wheelchair to admire and be inspirational, he having suffered horrendously in a diving accident when young. Norwegians also arrived, along with Swedes, all apparently speaking English from their cradles. Barbara Belt certainly visited, usually with her lovely daughters, she being my 'fixer' at Valle Gran Rey who had fixed almost everything. Tess and

Rick had arrived from England for a month, she brilliant with rope, and Rick, with Old English sheep-dog hair, happy in her company and ready to do whatever seemed necessary at the time.

Sometimes Barbara arranged that one or more of us should talk in town, tell of our plans and explain ourselves. Robin and I, for example, once addressed two schools. All its classes, whether young or younger, were identical in one respect. – question No.1 was always: 'Where's the toilet?' Barbara also drove me on my own to Valle Gran Rey Radio, a broadcasting station wishing for an interview, this to reach 'all' the modest community where we lived and worked. It was therefore with curiosity, along with some unnecessary arrogance, that I entered the 'Headquarters' of this organization. It proved to be two small rooms, their outer door open to the wider world where a game of dominoes was noisily proceeding along with raucous skateboarding by some youngsters up and down a set of concrete steps. Would I even hear the questions being put to me and might our audience, modest or minute, be able to disentangle all the various sounds? And what, for example, had been transmitted at the same time yesterday?

I gathered that a man aged ninety-three had told of some experience and I settled into a bone-hard chair, the better to learn of this geriatric happening. It transpired that a motorist, travelling at night along one of the many hairpin roads in that town's vicinity, had been irritated by headlights from the car behind him. He then became intrigued when those twin lights abruptly vanished. For a while he continued on his way until, with curiosity getting the better of him, he reversed uphill. Sure enough, further up that tortuous highway, there was a gap in the safety barrier. And, much to the driver's horror, he then saw a vehicle upside down some 200 metres below the road. Smoke and dust were still rising from the crash, and the man lost no time in contacting emergency services.

What these teams discovered, after lowering themselves down the near-precipitous slope, was astonishing. Not only was a very ancient man quite undamaged, and actually laughing, but his almost as elderly female accomplice was equally unhurt. It transpired that he was ninety-three, his companion was eighty-six, and both had braced themselves with their arms against the vehicle's inside roofing while it had tumbled from on high.

'She's my new girlfriend,' said the man to the police, 'and I'm so glad she's not hurt.'

The girlfriend in question not only affirmed her unbroken state but admitted that the two of them had only recently become a duo. Together, most joyfully and arm in arm, they were then helped and pulled up the terrifying slope, with occasional sadness being expressed that their vehicle might as well be left in place, it being without value any more.

'Now,' said my interviewer/studio manager/general hand, 'what's this story of yours about a raft?'

By this time all arrogance had gone, quite torn to shreds. At least the man did not ask about the toilet, but I really cannot remember what else was said, either by him or me during the interview, with my tale of such little consequence when set beside the previous day's extraordinary offering. I did not even care whether anyone heard our words, hoping their extreme unimportance would be drowned by the considerable banging of little tiles along with the happy yells of skateboarders so very close at hand.

Back at the construction site, when each lunch hour arrived, someone – such as Robin – assessed the workforce number and went off to buy sufficient food. Work surfaces then made good tables on which we sawed baguettes, axed tomatoes into quarters, chiselled strips of cheese and Swiss Army knifed practically everything else while feasting happily. These were good times, with only occasional twinges of concern that it was a trans-oceanic vessel which we were laughing about, and hammering into place. If the person next to you is a tattooed tapestry, decorated excitingly from top to toe, it is difficult to remember that she and you are engaged on crucial work, akin to folding up a parachute. It certainly should not matter whether Lise or Carine had brought Toblerone that day, even if the fact earned comment at the time. So did almost everything, with jest and banter never far away. Without this so very varied assistance, quite unforeseen when I had hazarded 3 January as completion date, I doubt that we would have been ready by 15 February, Spain's absolute cut-off date after which no form of sailing vessel is permitted to leave until hurricanes have well and truly ended blowing at the Atlantic's other side. No wonder that we were very grateful for all these volunteers who thoroughly deserved their crusty bread overladen with cheese, ham, fruit and pickle.

There was only one dissenting individual in all this harmony and we even had a name for him – Klepto. This middle-aged German visited our site most regularly. He did not simply look, as many did. Instead he stalked, much like some wading bird intent upon edibles half-hidden by its feet. Every now and then this human visitor would pounce, perhaps upon a slice of wood, a bit of cloth, a discarded length of wire. One day, when David had been using such a length as a crude but helpful measurer, the German had snatched that very piece, thus adding to his hoard. David, putting out his hand to find the foot-long length of wire where he had left it, was casually and then more actively mystified by its abrupt disappearance. I, having observed the villainy, therefore shouted that Klepto was at fault, enabling David to retrieve his precious length from that man's outer pocket. This was, I thought, too much. Stoppers and those who merely stared were all very well. Earnest questioners were not resented, although often time-consuming, but the acquisitive removal of bits and pieces, such as those still in use, was more than a touch excessive. I therefore banished the burgling man, almost fluently, but my demand was clear. Klepto should go and, if possible, not come back again.

'*Raus*,' I even said, much as prison guards in old films shout at every British prisoner of war who is being laggardly.

So he went, muttering as he departed, and we were much relieved. The starers continued, along with all the questioners, but at least our active construction area was no longer searched for bits and pieces striking one man's thieving fancy. In fact we saw him no more until, one day, he levered himself from his little car while holding a package in his hands. Of course we were curious before being amazed by that thing's contents. They formed a model raft, excitingly made from lengths of wood and cloth and wire, most of which we recognized from earlier working days.

Humiliation tends not to come in modest doses and all of us – particularly myself – were sickened by memory of that model raft's creator and his dismissal from our scene. He did not let us keep that diminutive, well-made thing, despite our grasping hands, and no doubt it now rests upon a mantelpiece back in the homeland. It surely reminds him of his enthusiastic labour while on a recent Canary island holiday and also of a group of Britons who, for reasons he could never fathom, actively prevented him from further gathering of various bits, all offcuts from their work. In particular, there was a piece of wire, about thirty centimetres long, that would have served him and his hard-won model most excellently.

The planned completion date of 3 January became 13 January, when everything was finally ready for the launch and baptism. It was therefore occasion to summon Nicasio once again. This time two machines, one even bigger than its colossal predecessor, were considered necessary for the task of shifting some twelve tons of raft (oh farewell Tom Sawyer, yet again) from construction site to a sloping ramp and finally to sea. Nicasio and an accomplice gazed at each other, gesticulated when necessary, and also mouthed information without a word being actually pronounced. There was smoke everywhere, and great noise, and pairs of wheels often rising high above the ground, with one machine pulling and the other pushing while poor *Antiki* was made to move for the first time in its life. The exhausts snorted at so much labour but, inch by inch, the ninety-metre distance from site to sea was steadily accomplished. Very soon – well, a couple of hours later – our splendid creation was poised at the very top of that ever-so-handy and enticing ramp, thus mimicking some diver about to plunge from a high board to a placid pool waiting down below. It was a tense moment, but Nicasio and his mate thought nothing of it. Both of them then switched off their engines before vanishing in a little van, having apparently decided that launchings occur at the starting of a day and not at its conclusion. Time, therefore, for a beer.

Came the dawn, with much talk from all the security men, from passers-by, from harbour officialdom and everyone with speech about the high tide mark. It was best, they all decided, if the ramp's distant end was as near the water level as the changing tide made possible, but there was total disagreement about when that time might be.

'Wait a bit more,' vied with, 'Do it now,' and, 'Check the tables with Tenerife.'

Such monkey chatter was of zero interest to Nicasio, the senior machine man now re-arrived. With a stab at his starter button, the familiar belch of blackness from his exhaust, a little shove from his colossal bucket scoop and *Antiki* sped down the slope most obediently to float quite perfectly. Game, set and a beautiful conclusion to all that talk. Our raft looked exquisite; in fact miraculous. We had made bets between ourselves how high would be the water level on the four basic two-foot pipes, and optimism won the day. Twelve tons of weight were as nothing, or so it seemed. Most audibly I shouted, 'West Indies here we come!' Most silently I prayed that restrictive officialdom would keep away, that the Spanish authorities would maintain a blind eye over our activities, that money from cash dispensers might be forthcoming once again, that good weather would bless our undertaking, and the hugely successful launching would be followed by an embarkation no less good.

'Why is it floating?' asked an onlooker.

'Why indeed!' I responded, entirely happily.

We wanted a woman to perform the naming ceremony. Already acquired was a bottle of 'champagne', this thought to be a snip at three euros, and we prepared an iron fastening upon the mast to make sure libation occurred on cue. There were suitable females among our gathering but we had decided that a handsome councillor, one of those in charge of the delightful community where we lived and worked, would be more apt. We therefore invited and she arrived in a severe two-piece trouser suit. This excellent representative of VGR authority was soon scampering down the somewhat dodgy makeshift ladder we had fashioned for access from quay to waiting raft. We then all hushed while formal words were read which loudly requested assistance for the brave souls 'who would sail in her'. The bulbous bottle was soon handed over, this tied to the mast by cord. Our baptizer took the thing, tested it for weight, pulled back her arm to make us think of discus-throwing in old Olympia, and soon threw determinedly. Plainly, as we all realized, three-euro champagne bottles are not made with lightweight glass, and she had to throw again. The noise of bottle against iron was very loud, but still the deed remained undone. I do not know how she behaves when sitting in the council chamber but we each acquired an inkling when this councillor, confronted by one bottle's unwelcome opposition, took the insult personally. Throw number four was frightening, but less so than number five. As for number six, that would have launched a super-tanker, with glass and drink suddenly distributed almost everywhere. The mast may have quivered from the assault, but we crew certainly shook with joy before giving her happy kisses and then watching – with admiration – how she in her smart suiting scampered up the ladder to greet the town's official band, still in mid-blow with all its trumpeting. It was a very happy ceremony, and may the raft *Antiki* meet fair wind plus good fortune wherever she will go.

The date was 14 January – not bad when considering that I had estimated 3 January before we had even arrived at the islands – but launching is different from departing. There was still the loading to be achieved. All the food boxes, all the water, everyone's personal possessions and everything for the voyage had to go down that rickety ladder, save for water going onboard by handy pipe. Much weight went down with, astonishingly, no change in what we called the Plimsoll line. Our raft did not seem to lower itself one bit, despite the extra tonnage heaved, and lowered, and finally stored onboard. Of course all this labour used up more days, as did bad weather and contrary wind.

'It's getting even further from 3 January,' said David, more than once.

The third day of the year had, for him, been carved in stone. For me it had only been a guesstimate (such a handy word), a rough idea, a token of intent, a heartfelt desire and not a thing of certainty. Ah well, there was plenty to worry about without caring that 3 January did eventually become a launch date of 14 January, with the final tasks more or less complete by 20 January, and then a wait until 30 January when the wind had swung around to being beneficial rather than plain wrong. It was then sixty-nine days since Tony (crucial helper),

Trial raft in Melbourne

Early design of raft layout

(Robin Batchelor)

Dave working on
the raft

Raft construction in
Valle Gran Rey

(Robin Batchelor)

John tests the rigging

(Robin Batchelor)

Antiki crew just before departure

(Robin Batchelor)

Antiki on launch day

Antiki in Valle Gran Rey harbour

Anthony finally puts to sea in his raft

Antiki heads south away from Valle Gran Rey

The crew soon settle in to life on the ocean wave

John and Andy take a dip in The Atlantic

Andy catches a Dorado but Anthony insists it is returned to its family following *Antiki*

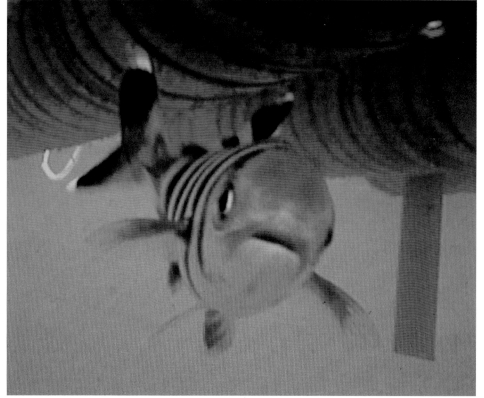

Dave captures a Dorado with his underwater camera

The steering sweep helps guide the raft

Robin (no less crucial enthusiast about everything), the container and myself had arrived at Valle Gran Rey. How long should it take to make a raft ready to confront whatever the Atlantic has up its sleeve? I did not know but thought – and knew – we had done well.

This frequent talk about 3 January had made me realize – while still constructing – that I had better clarify our intended destination. There were many reasons why I wanted to do the trip but only one end point had ever been linked to those various wishes. Eleuthera was the island where those two lifeboat survivors had landed in October 1940 after their seventy days afloat. I wished that our venture, a mere seventy-one years later, should also encounter land where those two young men's ordeal had finally been ended. Its latitude and longitude were well known, with one small and stunted tree still growing just by the actual spot. A 1940 photograph of their beached boat showed this wizened thing, and photos taken in the current century confirmed that it still lived. My wish to land at that very spot was partly to remind everyone of the merchant marine's wartime courage but also to prove that rafts can be successfully navigated, being not entirely subject to the direction of wind and current. Landing somewhere else would be a success – sailing a raft across the Atlantic – but not the achievement I desired.

Therefore, and in the dying days of 2010, I had called a meeting of the crew who would be travelling on the raft. This could not happen until John Russell had arrived after Christmas (having abandoned his legal chair) but, with him by then firmly one of the party, the meeting could go ahead. Instead of the normal banter so enjoyable when a group decides that a day's work has been completed, and is welcoming beer for all it has to give, I spoke as if this were some committee meeting working its way through an agenda.

53

'Are we all agreed that Eleuthera will be our destination, preferably at the very beach where Tapscott and Widdicombe landed in 1940?'

There were murmurs of assent from around the table before this unanimity was sealed with further sips of beer. Reaching Eleuthera, as against some nearer West Indian island, meant travelling further and taking more time before the journey was completed, but that was my definite wish. The crew had now formally agreed to take this extra time and sail the further distance. Rafting across the Atlantic was my idea and I had paid for it. Therefore I could command the destination. All four of us were now committed to the great idea, so it was 'Eleuthera here we come'. The plan was not hard-wired, as if some legal document, but was set as firmly as I – as all four of us – could arrange.

The West Indies are, of course, a very mixed assembly. Some are much nearer Africa than others, with Barbados and the Leewards among the closest. My longed-for destination, Eleuthera in the Bahamas, was among the furthest, being some 800 miles north-west of the nearest chunks of land. This further group of islands was also harder to achieve and involved greater sailing potential than a raft – than our raft – might be able to employ. Nevertheless we had all made the compact and had agreed about Eleuthera. It was our destination and we had nowhere else in mind. That point had been settled, or so I thought, as those earliest rafting days passed by.

5

Our cabin on *Antiki* was fourteen feet long, eight feet wide and eight feet tall in the centre. There was a separate compartment curtained off at the rearward end, containing two bunks which were used by John, Andy and David in rotation. My bunk was forward of these others, and shared one cabin side with the electronics gear. On the opposing portion was the cooking equipment, along with the cooker itself, this fed with butane from an outside supply. We chose to keep watch from 9.30 p.m. to 7.30 a.m., adjusting 'raft time' gradually to keep in touch with the sun's alterations as we slowly travelled west. The further we travelled towards the famous Indies, the earlier grew the time that our clocks and watches should have shown. Andy had a magnificent timepiece on his wrist which was able to tell far more than time, such as our course and North's location, but it loathed being asked to change the position of its hands by any amount, let alone by one whole hour. Therefore, with Andy reluctant to bring this Little Ben into line with the sun, we were usually late in doing so. His chronological bit of wizardry was also waterproof for many fathoms, its weight surely urging the owner downwards should he chance to swim with the thing still strapped around his wrist.

I was given the 9.30 p.m. to midnight stint, another form of kindness because my night-time sleep could then be an unbroken eight-hour span. In practice, and at each switching hour, the consideration proved better still. Manoeuvring by two others, one leaving, one arriving, one adding clothes and one discarding them, tended to nudge my reposing form, this then sighing very happily that more sleep was still my due. When 7.30 a.m. was reached the dawn watchkeeper tended to stay outside, waiting for whoever first felt like surfacing. These two then chatted, and they did so more determinedly when man No.3 arrived. As for man No.4 – my recumbent self – he could continue doing nothing, save listen distractedly and wonder, not for the first time, at the ability of humans to talk without having anything to say.

Breakfast occurred at 10 a.m. or so.

'Where are the Coco Pops?' was about as much intellectual achievement as could be expected at that hour, with Andy favouring this particular cereal. He and the others took great interest in the nutrition information printed on every packet.

'Good heavens!' Dr Andy might announce. 'These Pops contain barley. And three grams of fat if served with 125 millilitres of semi-skimmed milk. And five grams of salt but only six grams of protein.'

All riveting stuff! None of this stopped him from ladling the food into his mouth, or having a second go and being fascinated that his Coco bowl had similar calories to cornflakes but four times as much sugar, three times as much fat and five times as many saturates. John stayed aloof from such talk as his digestive system would not let him drink any form of milk with his choice of cereal. Instead he poured some juice upon his selection, making the food appear to the rest of us even less appealing than knowing of the twelve or eighteen ingredients involved in the creation of flaked corn or popped cocoa. Our milk was of the lasting kind, save – after this had all been consumed – when it became the very long-lasting kind, much favoured on La Gomera, a cow-less and almost goat-less place.

Breakfast was no occasion to ask out loud if Haydn was preferable to Mozart or Orwell of greater influence than Koestler in
criticizing communism. We were too deeply involved in the
nitty-gritty of life itself, each cereal's 'Recommended Daily
Allowances' that previous generations – poor things – had
never even known.

Lunchtime talk was more random, as was the problem of
balancing 'spreads' either upon crumbling bread or on bread
planks whose crumbling powers had long since vanished. It
was a meal combining laziness with skill. Find your desired pot
of spread, scoop some of its contents, balance these upon crust
or crumb, and carry the offerings mouthwards with minimum
delay and spillage. Fingers played important roles, these also
spread as with bread, and therefore sucked clean with clever
mouth-work while the associated crumb and crust were similarly consumed. All rather tricky. I cannot remember much
talk during lunch, with munching and ingesting more than
sufficient as a task.

Supper was the culinary highlight of the day and even occa-
sioned a preliminary ceremony. We four, most solemnly,
dropped the previously gentle form of inactivity, whether reading, wave-watching or just resting before moving nearer to the
raft's apex. There we made ourselves comfortable, by sitting or
merely leaning, and all four most earnestly watched the sun go
down at the hour it chose. We even gave it marks (out of ten),
with ten – in a curmudgeonly way – never actually donated. A
really good sunset needed clouds in all the right places to
create shafts of sunlight sprouting forth. David said he had
heard these called 'Jesus's fingers' but the phrase never caught
on with the four of us. Instead we were content to admire and
gasp and wholeheartedly enjoy. From top to bottom the solar
vanishing takes 3.5 minutes and we never abandoned the deck
until the show was ended. Not once have I ever watched

sunsets from my home in Acton. And only once did we fail to see one when in mid-Atlantic.

On that occasion we had, as always, been alert to the heavenly changes going on near the horizon. Trade-wind clouds were all there, each mimicking the shapes of their neighbours, thus making more of a cavalcade than the ordinary kind of sky when cotton-wool puffs of cumulus seem scattered rather randomly. On that day we were expressing gratification out loud, and even critically, when one portion of the sky became slightly fuzzy. This would never do! Why such mismanagement and so suddenly? Why indeed – until pennies dropped among the four of us. This display was prerequisite to a squall and the thing was heading our way. In my gibbon-fashion I swung swiftly to the cabin door, using anchor point after anchor point, and was totally inside when the rainstorm hit and caught the other three still hurrying for sanctuary with their drinks, books and cameras. What a transformation! What a near-immediate switch from perfect evening to torrential downpour. Wind blew seemingly from everywhere and tossed wetness at the raft with terrible aplomb. Andy tried to photograph the rain while the rest of us merely tried to understand how such an alteration could arrive so very hastily. It was a show of force from the elements, a reminder of who or what was truly in control, a flexing of other muscles, an enlightenment of fact we should never have forgotten. We would be as nothing if the opposing strengths chose to show their full-scale opposition to our endeavour. We would be as mincemeat, very speedily. We might even be overturned.

'That was some squall,' said the others.

'It *is* some squall,' I added, as the thing was still most visible.

Its pelting water, falling so overwhelmingly, was then as suddenly vanished as it had so immediately begun. The whole sky soon brightened and became its normal self again, with the former savagery and violence nowhere to be seen. The thing had gone completely and it was no wonder that yachts can be overturned by such sudden vehemence. As for rafts, and our one in particular, *Antiki* behaved brilliantly, much as it had done thus far in our considerable voyaging. I had thought an over-turning might be possible – which would explain why some rafts are never seen again – and I knew, for sure, that an over-turned raft could never be set to rights once more. Mast, spar, rigging, sail and cabin would each combine to hinder such an act, whatever the waves might do. As for the crew, they would be dying or dead if their craft turned turtle. That seemed to me a certainty.

'So how's supper,' said someone by way of interruption.

This meal would be, almost certainly, a mélange, a pot-pourri, a hash, a splash, a mash, its titles varying more than the offerings, with everything firmly based upon potatoes (in the earliest days) or pasta, rice and soya. The potatoes grew soft with time, and we were intrigued by the wording on their sack that they came from Essex. We later wrote to the exporters, calling ourselves inverted Walter Raleighs by taking potatoes back from the Old World to the New, but never received reply. Anyway, on all their starch, some taste and substance was added from the wide selection of tinned extras, such as tomatoes (often), beans (oftener), peas (oftenest), fish (occasionally), meat (rarely) and novelties (never known as such after the first few days). It was hard for the three cooks taking turns to be creative and therefore produce *Hash Surprise*, because we consumers knew the possibilities as well as they did. Extra taste could be administered from bottles and cubes and spreads, as and how each day's chef thought fit, that is if he actually thought when slooshing, crumbling, pouring or dolloping drips and drabs of variety upon that evening's offering. Suffice to say, whether a squirt of ketchup or dab of Marmite was actually improvement, everything was subsequently eaten, with every panful being consumed, however impossible this seemed at the outset. At supper time's conclusion each chef could relax, knowing he had fully assuaged considerable appetite.

It was then occasion for one more preliminary before the evening's entertainment. Whether each of us did the washing up or towelled things dry or merely passed plates from one hand to another, we all gathered to see if the dorados were still there. Of course they were, their fantastic blue so much more conspicuous at night-time than by day. Almost exclusively these fishes favoured the starboard side, and we tried to reason why. With each evening's inspection we saw – almost always – a greater number than twenty-four hours earlier, and of course rejoiced. In size they were at least a metre long but it was hard to tell. The books made them appear ugly, with a bulbous forehead above a downturned mouth, but we thought them exquisite and were ludicrously proud that they had arrayed themselves to keep us company. They made us feel – they certainly made me feel – as if we were part of some cavalry charge, not quite in line as with drilled soldiery but spurring to catch up should they ever slip behind. Every now and then one would leap out of the water, and then fall back again with a noisome flop. Of course we all then shouted with extra vigour but each leap failed to affect any other fish in the leaper's neighbourhood. All response came vociferously from us. Dorados 'generally hunt in packs, having first been attracted to floating debris', or so stated books. Not a bit of it, we each concurred. They were attracted to our most excellent raft, and did so in steadily greater numbers as our voyage continued. (Most oddly they are also called 'mahi,' which is the word for fish in Farsi, a curious fact I knew!)

'I think there were ten this evening,' someone might say.

'I'm sure it was eleven,' would say someone else, almost inevitably.

It was then occasion for in-cabin entertainment, and sometimes this was cards. Plainly, during the long winter nights in Western Canada, they play a lot of cards, as Andy was never short of some new game such as Queen of Hearts, Sevens or merely Thirty-One. Intelligence was occasionally required, and Andy did best of all having learned a thing or two while snow was silently filling his driveway yet again. It was the subsequent language that intrigued me most.

'Why, you shit-faced turd,' muttered someone. 'You knew I had the Ace.'

Andy would smile nastily while 'crap' and 'creep' and 'goon' were aimed his way by others, these players prevented from going Out by the bastard's loathsome style of play. The ripostes used by all of us were extraordinarily foul and somewhat childish, but never caused offence. They were, I think, the inevitable consequence of bottling up so much thought during every raft-borne day. If someone had been modestly annoying, by word or act, it was quite lovely to call him something execrable when the time was right, to say those words straight into his face, and not only get away with it but make the others laugh. How could he be quite so shitty? So turd-like? So crapulous? Very easily, so it seemed.

Andy was one of the only two determined fishermen onboard. David was the other, and both had insisted upon the purchase (more back pocket, more euros, more frowning wonder at further necessities) of hooks and line and lures. One day Andy thought the time was right to test his fishing skills, these no doubt honed either on or in or by splendid Albertan rivers when surface ice had become water once again. In any case, and on the raft, he laid out the purchased equipment with care, as if some medical operation was about to be performed. Eventually, and while the rest of us settled down to watch, he dangled a suitably enticing and glittering thing at the end of a length of line. Our doctor's face took on that tranquil look which fishermen employ, particularly to ward off those who might ask about their 'catch' and also to imply they do not really expect anything to be hooked that hour, that day, that week. Resignation is the word and, being infectious, it affected the rest of us as well.

Therefore surprise was felt all round when the line suddenly went taut. Advice about what best to do then filled the air, everyone – save for Andy – giving urgent voice. Quietly he disdained it all, and very soon he had a large, and extremely handsome, fish upon his lap. This creature flapped relentlessly, being blatantly ungrateful for the rapid change in its circumstance. Andy sat motionless as if helplessly watching some unruly child tossing everything from its pram. Plainly our fisherman was having thoughts and the rest of us were quietened before such obvious contemplation. Silence was often Andy's way. He did not jump to conclusions; he steadily approached them. Something would emerge eventually, and that something then did so when its time was due.

'Is this fish on my lap a kind of cousin to our dorados?'

In our various ways, and longing to contribute to his brown study, we each agreed that the creature was 'a kind of cousin', a 'fellow fish', a 'definite member of the tribe'.

'In which case,' announced Andy, 'I cannot possibly eat it. Not only is it related but, as I've learned from the books, dorados mate for life.'

Then, without waiting for additional remarks from his three ever-ready advisers, he stood and tossed his unruly catch back into the turbulent sea. We all watched the presumed meal vanish instantly, proving it was still absolutely full of life. Its experience of living in another medium for a little while, this so energetically and flappingly resented, had apparently done no harm at all. And that was that. Andy had given his firm opinion which nobody could deny. Hooked fish were off the menu, and were off for good. The man who had been most outspoken about our steady lack of 'real food', which meant steaks and other forms of meat, had chosen to deny the very flesh which an ocean could so easily supply.

'You see,' added Andy, 'the fact of dorados mating for life makes it all much worse.

'I'll stick to sardines,' he then concluded, thus stressing the subject's closure, 'because they're already dead.'

'And have had their heads chopped off,' added John, thus clinching the argument.

Very dead these certainly were, with tin after tin of them just waiting in a nearby bin. The topic of eating fish fresher by very many months (or years?) was never raised again, with such a firm opinion expressed by one of us being totally sufficient. Even when tucking into the little fishy and tinned offerings, so bathed in alien olive oil, no one dared to reopen the discussion. Even if still bleeding from de-lidding yet another array of headless cousins, each with one thousandth of the flesh that had existed, so shiningly fresh, upon our doctor's lap. Much to everyone's surprise (including his, I suspect) the fishing tackle never re-emerged to be successful once again.

'You what?' our later questioners were to say. 'You never caught or ate a single fish during all your weeks at sea?'

'Of course we could catch fish,' we'd reply, 'and were successful.'

As an answer it usually failed to satisfy, but was the truth. Perhaps, and in Western Canada, there is now a framed photograph, conspicuously hung upon a surgery wall, of one medical fisherman glancing happily downwards at a magnificently shiny and edible three-pounder resting on his lap.

'Oh that? Funny you should notice that! Yup, that's me, and that's one fine fish I caught on a lure out in the Atlantic. Yup, it was actually my first.'

True, every single word. It was also true that not one of us ever disputed Andy's dictatorial right to cancel fresh fish from our menu. We were not vegetarians. We happily opened can after can of the smaller fishes, along with occasional slabs of tinned mackerel, but we never did eat any form of cousin, younger by months or more. It was as if we were desperate to avoid any possible dissent, hating the thought of opposition, maintaining peace whatever the cost – however much everyone would have welcomed a bit of fresh fish from time to time (such as most evenings). I had thought, when Andy made his pronouncement, that David was about to speak but nothing actually emerged. His good friend Andy had voiced opinion and that was good enough for him. It was also good enough for all. The subject was dead, and no readier for further consideration than each threesome of *sardinos* packed in tins were capable of further life.

6

My reasons for embarking on the raft idea – sounding so similar, said almost everyone, to 'daft idea' – and at my time of life, were extremely mixed and difficult to disentangle; but, without doubt, 'my dead' were in there somewhere and quite distinct from all the other impulses to travel the Atlantic. This phrase had been used by Spitfire pilot Richard Hillary to justify his writing *The Last Enemy*, that bestseller he created about lengthy Battle of Britain days, and the short lives that these consumed. Despite the differences between his experiences and mine (in a subsequent century no less), similar feelings were aroused in me when great companions so frequently disappeared – not felled by bullets but by the still more lethal business of growing old. In recent years I had lost so many of my closest friends, vanishing in their nasty wooden boxes either to be consumed by flames or whatever soil dictates.

'If I had any decency I'd be dead,' said Dorothy Parker (when aged seventy). 'Most of my friends are.'

Too true. If anyone lives to reach the average age for their upbringing and style of life, half of their contemporaries will have gone. This arithmetic is most straightforward, being as dependable as the maths in 1940 when some 10 per cent of pilots failed to return from every flight. My particular assortment of old chums are not dying as flies are said to do, but are making quite a shot at it. Their several vanishings each remind me, yet again, that there is something about long-standing friendships that cannot be duplicated by new acquaintances, however admirable these newcomers may be. One of my oldies, with an extremely unsteady hand, had written to me on one dreadful day of his quadruple bypass operation which had left three of his arteries still quite blocked.

'Things are going from bad to worse,' George had written to me two weeks before he died, and, 'if this is Addio, it is with fervent gratitude that we met.'

Each rereading of his words brings on misery and tears, with that letter's desperate p.s. telling how his wife had already 'gone on her own into Alzheimer's miserable retreat.' Half a century earlier I had been best man at their wedding and now, of course, I was loathing their departures. Were all my long-term friends, such fine people, being truly vanquished? Was there nothing left of them, of all the former laughter and their longings, of their wisdom and their wonder? More to the point, if I could open a coffin lid and those inside could speak, they would surely ask what I was doing with my time, with my pair of legs and with the planet still in all its excellence which we had jointly so enjoyed. To say that I was pottering would undoubtely arouse their scorn.

'Surely you remember Sicily,' George might then have added, 'where we had worshipped at Greek temples, roared words in the ancient theatres of Syracuse and Taormina, taken fourteen-hour train journeys from south to south-east of that island, and thought everything we saw quite miraculous, the men sitting nearby as fellow travellers, with their buttoned-up and collarless shirts, their black-clothed women chattering unendingly and all the equally ceaseless joy of vines and olives just beyond our train's considerable window panes.' Fourteen hours were nothing like long enough for us, notably when our compartment of companions let us share their suitcased food, this sufficient to feed a regiment.

There was also James who saw beauty everywhere, not only in the majesty of the Renaissance, but in the manner that modern labourers piled their bricks, or their families hung laundry on makeshift lines between quattrocento and today, or the young men who scootered on Vespas and Lambrettas with their sitting-sideways female companions who knew absolutely about the bodies that were them – and which, so soon, would be clothed in black. He and I had once canoed (in a military Folbot 'borrowed' earlier from an *Inglese capitano*) down 200 miles of Tyrrhenian coastline, coming ashore each evening, cooking our pasta on spitting driftwood, relishing the raffiad bottles of coarse red wine, sleeping where we lay and only setting sail when wind arrived each subsequent midday to blow us further south.

At the village of Talamone it was occasion for James's shorts, their seams by now quite unattached, to be set to rights. And so they were, in situ, by an exquisite fourteen-year-old, whose delicate but probing little fingers were guided by those of her twenty-eight-year-old mama, and with everything gleefully admired by a nonna not one day older than forty-two. (Just why, oh why, did we ever leave that place? It had everything mere humans could actually desire.) At Fiumicino we disembarked, took a bus to nearby Rome, failed initially to enter St Peter's (our clothing considered unimpressive) and then had laughed enthusiastically when a nearby newsvendor kitted us out with the very same outfit that, in Procrustean fashion, fitted all in need. Great days, near permanent magic and beauty everywhere!

But James, dying at the decent age of eighty-six from a failing heart which made it difficult for that energetic individual even to leave his bed, was not alone.

'What did you do, John, before coming to Oxford from Australia?'

'I studied the quokka.'

'And how did you find your quokka?'

'Well, you look for potoroos, and then you'll discover quokka.'

How can such an individual not become a friend at once? And then stay, as a good mate, until his closing time? They say that double pneumonia is the old man's friend, in that it kills swiftly without much pain, but it is less welcomed by each old man's long-lasting human friends who hear, by phone or ordinary word of mouth, that a buddy for over sixty years is suddenly no more, having gone most unexpectedly.

I met Philip, no less memorably, on the back of a people-laden truck slowly lurching its way through a remote part of Brazil's up-country Mato Grosso state.

'Do you realize,' he said, almost the moment I had clambered onboard, 'that the recurrent laryngeal nerve goes from the human brain right around the aorta by the heart before travelling back up to reach the larynx, which means an unnecessary and extra foot or so with humans and some thirteen extra feet with the giraffe?'

I knew nothing of the sort, save that another great companion had come my way, not only for the continuation of that horrendous track carved through equatorial forest but for the remainder of his days. When aged ninety-five he had been wheeled round a van Gogh exhibition just one week before he too succumbed. I bet, should others have sidled up to have a word that day with the wheelchair's occupant, they too would have been enchanted by some chunk of information which just had to be expressed. That was always Philip's way, with the facts being medical, geographical, archaeological, artistic, ethnographical or even involving mountaineering. Of course he did good work by his job of doctoring but he also used that early training to get him where he wished to go, such as towards a recently contacted tribe or victims of some new disease or people living at great altitude. If I prized open his coffin lid he would ask less about what I was doing (or failing to do) but about what we should both be doing without delay, even if this meant bouncing on the back of some crowded and overladen truck.

How Roy had become a press officer I do not know. His gift for concealing information was nil. His ability to appease his superiors rather than journalists was also modest, his favourite story being of the day in 1957 when Windscale's No.1 nuclear reactor surprised everyone by catching fire before distributing radioactive elements, such as caesium-137 and iodine-101, around much of Cumbria.

'Tell them nothing,' said Roy's superior.

'What? Nothing at all about our biggest nuclear accident?'

'That's right, Herbert. Not a thing.'

Roy was a man to set you laughing even if beginning 'I was on the M1 yesterday.' This most tedious of roads is hardly the cat's whiskers for instant levity, but in Roy's hands it could have you on the floor so very smartly. What was he – of all people – doing, or were all such friends doing, so tightly encased within their wooden boxes? And what was I doing, treasuring these memories, while standing on my own two feet (when not sitting down) and mouthing farewells to such great people inside yet another unlovely crematorium? I had better justify myself, and do something worthy of the extra lease of life. Hence one more reason for going to sea, perhaps the most powerful of them all. My personal dead were urging me onwards, just as Richard Hillary's youthful dead had been encouraging him so powerfully and silently, even helping to kill him in the end. (His burned hands were not up to the task of flying a twin-engined plane, particularly if being flown at night.) The Battle of Britain slaughter had been horrendous, with so many young lives cut down. The one occurring at the end of life was being a deal more devastating by killing everyone.

All these individuals, along with others, had been marker-points in my life. It was not so much the length of time that I had known them but that they had surfaced at crucial moments in my personal development. George, for example, had told me to watch *The Tempest*, this play being performed by Oxford undergraduates in Worcester College's magnificent gardens. It was a supreme production, particularly with Ariel receiving his freedom at the play's conclusion and then running across the lake in exultation – yes, *running* across the darkened water – before ascending skywards to release a thunderbolt. All pure magic and quite brilliant (however much we later learned of assembled and floating trestle tables over which his feet could run, plus a form of stairway pushed upwards and into place after the sun had set).

'O brave new world, That has such people in't.'

It may be arrogant – or plain wrong – to say so, but we, when young and immediately after World War Two, did feel quite new. Such dreadful killing – of fifty million in those six years, for heaven's sake! – had to stop. I had watched that Shakespeare play with a German girl, her father still imprisoned within the Soviet Union, and we two assuredly felt new. Without money, or the necessary permissions as a student, I had meant to install her with a friend, only for her husband to refuse. 'There will be no Germans staying in our house,' he had demanded. I do not remember where my German ended up, but do know for sure that we two from two nations did feel part of a brand-new world, with people such as us within it. Perhaps each new generation determinedly thinks this way, with all the outspoken stridency of youth, and we certainly believed it in the later 1940s after the earlier 1940s had been brought – at long last – to a peaceful end. We had joined, and were very much part of, a brave new world and did, in consequence, feel superior.

People born a generation later may be sympathetic to this post-war notion but it is not a part of them. We can all wonder at the dumb obedience of the troops who had walked across no-man's-land on 1 July 1916 before being mown down in their thousands, but those of us born later cannot truly understand all that lethal loyalty. Thus it was with my threesome of raft companions, each of them a generation younger than myself. We were apart where it mattered most. They knew more recent things which I did not. They knew the 1990s and the early 2000s which had somehow disinterested me.

On the raft we were most suited to each other with shared novelties, like picking up the flying fish which had come onboard at night, like watching waves trying to follow suit, like being at sea-level turbulence and yet not inundated, like rafting, which was something so overwhelmingly new for every one of us. Waves, somewhat inevitably, were a constant source of wonder.

They may look like water, and be composed of water, but are only quantities of energy which are passing through because the water stays intact, more or less in the same place. Each consignment of power is perhaps travelling for some 10,000 miles from Antarctica up to the Arctic, and it may take a couple of weeks or more for the journey to be completed. The actual water which it meets, and which can be so devastating, is only travelling in an ellipse and not forwards, as might seem to be the case. Waves are not immortal because both surface tension and gravity are steadily trying to flatten them. In fact they are much like sound going through the air. It is only the vibration which arrives elsewhere and not the air through which it travels. Little energy is lost during a wave's passage; hence the enormous distances they can voyage from start to finish. Considerable energy is involved, a fact we rafters realized vehemently, with our relentless motion up and down. To comprehend that energy we estimated how much power was necessary to heave up such a quantity of water for ten feet or so. The thought of doing that tremendous lifting – and every six seconds or so – made us appreciate the energy involved as, oh so casually, we moved about our craft, perhaps occasionally mentioning that 'the waves are big today'.

A wave dies, which every toddler knows when running back and forth half-hoping to be 'caught', just before it meets the shore. It first rises up when drag decreases the lower portion's speed. As the upper portion is encountering no such resistance it therefore 'breaks', much to the joy of surf-riders if big enough or the lesser pleasure of mere swimmers who leap up when waves arrive. Eventually the formerly mighty thing dribbles up the shore, perhaps reaching further than some predecessor or, more probably, less far. So what has happened to all the energy which had been travelling for the previous two weeks? It cannot have vanished because energy does not disappear. Instead it is dissipated via noise and also by moving material such as sand. In short it has done work, with each of those two tasks being great consumers of the power.

It so happened that a massive tsunami hit Japan while we were rafting, and doubts were expressed elsewhere about our safety. Such destructive waves do indeed travel great distances – and at speeds measured in hundreds of miles per hour – but tsunami forces are dependent upon the ocean's depth. Our raft's location at the time happened to be two or three miles above the seabed, as with most of the Atlantic, and any surface craft is unlikely to notice a tsunami's destructive energy passing by beneath. That force has to meet shallower water before its energy becomes more concentrated. It then hurls itself upon the land to cause massive destruction, and woe betide any raft – or other form of vessel – which happens to be near the coastline when such waves are, as it were, girding up their loins before becoming so horrendous in their devastation.

Onboard *Antiki* I think I was the major devotee of wave-watching, a synonym for doing nothing whatsoever. They were not all the same, far from it, any more than people's faces are the same, or leaves are, or roses or clouds or – I suppose – anything and everything once it has been accorded real examination. Each wave did appear unique, being quite distinct from its predecessors and the ones that followed. It almost seemed as if these slopes of water magnified themselves after seeing an object in their way. They then did their best to attack this object, such as an inoffensive vessel slowly travelling from east to west and perhaps the first such item to be encountered for several hundred miles. So they increased in bulk, rose up as if to subdue it, and then thrashed their way beneath it very noisily and as if angrily. Of course I watched and watched, seeing the impending fury and then the turbulent frustration as each wave assaulted our craft's lowest pipes before reappearing at our apex with lots of foam and froth. It finally galloped ahead of us at two or three times our speed. This process was unforgettable every time, and a relentless performance, with each new beginning trampling upon the coat tails of each and every ending. It was a sight of which I never tired, being permanently amazed how the raft lifted up its back end to escape each wall of water. Clever boxers evade each and every punch, however savage, by dodging all their fury. Our raft also sneered at each attack by jauntily rising above the wrath, expertly, neatly and certainly triumphantly. No wonder such a steady miracle was such a joy to watch.

It was definitely something to watch if one had need of what sailors call the 'heads'. Most luxuriously we had two onboard – or twice as many as a U-boat possessed where fifty men, far less privileged, usually saw the second such item usurped for all-important food. During the raft's construction we could not agree from which directions waves might arrive during the voyaging, and compromised by installing one at the stern and the other halfway up the raft's port side. It was therefore occasion, when need arose, to take note of the actual situation. Was one of the pair of places quite untouched by water while the other was somewhat damp? Probably, and we would settle upon the dryness much as chickens arrange their backsides when about to straddle their clutch of eggs. It was all most comforting, to sit there in the warmth, to have bits of oneself enjoying the sun that rarely did so, to see the waves come and go, and know that life was good. To hand was a roll of paper, ready for its need. Trousers or shorts were at ankle height, relief was on its way and the occasion regularly provided a perfect sense of peace.

Or so we all thought when each of us savoured this form of solitude. On one day, hideously memorable – and certainly for me – one rogue wave observed a golden opportunity. It saw a human body arranged more nakedly than normal. It took note of his inability for swift escape, with his lengthy body hamstrung by its lowered clothing, this quite forbidding haste. The mound of approaching water quickly concentrated its quantity of energy before forming a truly massive wave and half-drowning the hapless individual. Its wetness wholly drenched his cumbersome anklet of trousers, pants and socks before deluging his unclothed frame. It even had water to spare for instantaneously transforming one dry roll of paper into a pathetically sodden sponge.

I was amazed by the immediate alteration of an earlier perfection. From being the most contented soul in the universe I had become a shivering thing, still holding in one hand, and most pointlessly, the former roll so important in this once-daily form of exercise. From glory to misery had been quicker than instantaneous, and the drenched roll went promptly overboard, accompanied of course by those four-letter words which

so sum up such a situation – and such a need – so very perfectly. Only laughter at my plight came from within the cabin
until, eventually, a brand-new roll was handed over to partner
a brand-new body, this now well washed from toe to top.

It does seem as if rogue is an appropriate word for the waves
– one in a hundred or one in a thousand – that are abnormal,
being part mischievous and part pure villainy. There is even
scientific argument that they are inevitable, with the increasing rarity of each type partnered by increasing force. Some
– the very rarest – are even said to sink major ships, there
being no other form of explanation for sudden disappear-
ances. Be that as it may, I was happy to think that – for the
modest price of a wettened body plus one wasted roll – my
rogue was of the smaller kind. But gentle days on the Atlantic
Ocean should never blind any voyager into believing that all
will stay well, at least until the other side is safely reached. As
with those times when aircraft engines seem to miss a beat, or
airframes clunk in novel fashion, one's heart is ready to jump
into one's mouth without delay should there be such sudden
cause. On *Antiki* I and the others appeared unaffected by my
brief soaking but I, for one, stayed apprehensive however calm
I may have looked. There was still a very long way to go.

On the other hand, and hitting me amidships from time to
time (much as the waves were doing), the raft was behaving
splendidly and we onboard were precisely where I – for sure –
had wished to be. We were in mid-Atlantic. There was no land
on either side for hundreds or thousands of miles. This was,
without doubt, another intensity. This was a 'deeper communion', with the wave cry, the wind cry and empty desolation.
How did Eliot get it all so right? And how had I done so right
in making the journey come to pass 'on the vast waters of the
petrel and the porpoise'? Yes, we were cleaning our teeth and
eating as if normality was in charge but the experience was
nothing of the sort. In silence I would spell it out – we were a

bunch of sane individuals on a group of pipes hoping to cross the broad Atlantic. And, most extraordinarily, we were crossing it on a thing we had put together without any experience of how such a thing should be. We were 'still and still moving', just as the poet said. We were explorers, however old. We were on a high and would be so for all the days to come. *Antiki* was on her way, along with the four of us. How amazing it all was.

I had not known what I was expecting or desiring when causing the raft to happen. Those back on land had presumed, quite wrongly, that I was anticipating storm. They imagined it was the danger that appealed. Far from it. Of course the Atlantic can get stormy, particularly during the northern hemisphere's summer months, but we had set off in January when winds were most likely to be calm. To start when they are most probable is like altering Russian roulette by having five bullets in the chamber rather than a singleton. There are charts which, after years of experience, indicate what is most likely by way of weather, of wind strength, of wind direction. They tell, all too clearly, of the quietest times and those that are most dangerous. They certainly told me that the northern winter, say November to January, is a good time to go. A storm is still feasible at any time of year but I wished to enjoy the trip, to think thoughts when zephyrs were in charge, to relish the fact of our situation – it possessing no one else for miles, no one to assist, nothing of any land and emptier of people in the neighbourhood than the peak of Everest. It was all so strange. It was mid-Atlantic. It was precisely where I wished to be.

7

By the third week of February we had reached latitude 19 North. More than that, we were trying to stick with it. This fact surprised some of those comfortably back at home.

'Why not 18 North?' formed the essence of their queries, with 18 being the conventional and speediest parallel for travelling from east to west within the famous 'trades'.

The answer lay with our wish, and certainly my wish, to reach the Bahamas, and that group's island of Eleuthera in particular. Sailing master David made the point that the further south we went (for the uninitiated, 18 North being below 19 North) the greater would be the distance for travelling up to meet our planned – and solemnly agreed in committee style – final destination. There were sixty nautical miles between each degree and these meant, in all certainty, at least two more days of sailing.

'It's better not to add on those days,' said David.

'Much better to stay as far north as is reasonably possible,' he added later on. 'And we must forget 18 North if we're aiming for Eleuthera,' he then solemnly declared.

As for myself, I am not experienced, but could not help getting the message embedded in his words – that time was crucial. This had its origins with that date of 3 January which I had proposed before even arriving at Valle Gran Rey. For me this had been a guess, something to aim for, but which David had viewed as the actual day of departure. Neither of us had appreciated that it might take several days of loading and packing between launching and sailing. Nor had we truly understood the fact that readiness to depart might not coincide with suitable weather. There was no point in a raft, however well prepared, setting off when the wind was contrary, no point whatsoever.

'So?' I said, sometimes out loud, to David after another day had passed before our voyage had begun.

'We're late,' said he.

'So?' I said again.

Our comments were perhaps not so clear-cut or concise, but that was the gist of them. As the journeying progressed, most of the domestic telephone calls he received from home seemed to add to his distress. Sometimes he even missed food following such a conversation. Nevertheless his onboard work did not suffer. If anything it became increasingly important – a form of distraction, an escape from reality, a departure of thoughts concerning home.

'My wife is missing me too much,' he said, quite frequently.

Convention tends to reverse this phrase, with wives being missed by absent husbands, but there was little we other three could do about this problem, save hope it would diminish. Certainly neither Andy nor John intervened with David's dilemma of wishing – when on a raft! – that everything would hurry up. There were still more than three-quarters of the journey to be achieved. At forty to fifty miles or so for each day's run, we would consume all of March and quite a bit of April before approaching any kind of land. That was the situation, whatever a wife might think, whatever we might do.

Other ships came and went, reminders of our pathetic haste. On 13 February *Ocean Trader* overtook us, heading for Brazil. Later that same day *Trident Endeavor* passed by, also en route to South America. We did not always see these ships, but our clever AIS device, using an aerial-to-aerial form of contact, told us all we needed to know about their course, their name and speed. It was very strange to learn of these other craft invading our space because they unhinged our sense of isolation. For day after day we had been on our own, and far more so than is ever possible with ordinary living. Then, and quite unsettling for equilibrium, a whole ship would suddenly appear in that colossal emptiness where we lived. Once or twice these other vessels would alter their course in our direction, creating a collision possibility – as David phrased it – where there had been nothing of the sort. At these times he therefore spoke to them via VHF Radio.

'Why have you altered course?'

'Hello *Antiki*. We see you are travelling at two knots, and must be in trouble. Perhaps we can help?'

'Hello *Ocean Trader* [or whoever]. We are a raft, and two knots is our speed. But thank you for your concern. Over.'

Our electronic print of information then showed them reverting to their earlier direction. In the main I did not welcome these intruders, for that is what I considered them to be. It was as if, having clambered to the top of Everest and revelling in its loneliness, another human suddenly arrives to invade one's silent reverie. The ships were from the real world, with timetables to keep, merchandise to offload and onboard people obeying other on-land people back in the communities which we had struggled so hard to leave behind us. I saw them as infringers, violators, transgressors, and was glad when they were out of sight, not only of us upon the raft but also of our cunning mast-high aerial.

Andy said he liked the ships, and certainly photographed them if at all possible. I think he welcomed the fact that, should any one of us be in trouble, other vessels would stop to render aid. That is the law of the sea. In a self-centred fashion, but with some reason, I presumed Andy was thinking of his onboard octogenarian as the likeliest candidate for assistance. For my part I had no idea what might be sufficient justification for halting a whole ship, for disrupting a busy schedule and costing all sorts of mega-money. A headache? No way. The black dog of depression (to borrow Churchill's phrase)? No way again, save that internal misery would certainly be eased, or modified, by the change in circumstance – with other people, another way of life and much convivial chat. A heart attack would or might suffice as a reason for requesting help, but would the transference – quite a heart-stopping procedure in itself – actually benefit the patient? There is much to be said for one's own bunk with all its faults rather than the greater comfort, once achieved, of being on an unknown ship destined for an unknown port and for whatever medical facilities this might provide.

I had once experienced the misery of kidney stones which had led to a four-bed hospital in mid-Brazil. There I had learned how dartboards must feel from all their puncturing before I summoned my body to get off the bed, hand over quite a bit of money and use an air-taxi before meeting again familiar friends who would merely let me be. A handy aphorism in this business of self-help: you have to be quite fit to experience illness – and to survive – in many a circumstance.

All such thoughts were vanquished after our thirteen-knot fellow travellers had travelled out of sight. The next newcomer did not cause a heart attack but certainly influenced that organ, making it pound most audibly. John was first to see, and then to shout. Despite being book bound for most off-duty hours, and with no additional eyes at the back of his head, he spotted more novelties than we other three combined. On that particular evening he was soon pointing and staring at a particular bit of sea. Nothing was there, save for a remembered noise which had plainly arisen from that area. This was fact

No.1 that we learned about whales. Their sound of blowing off is more immediately received than any sighting, with ears gathering information from everywhere and eyes never so all-embracing. John continued to point at the very spot where he had heard *and had then seen* the rounded back, a first in his experience.

'A white chin,' said John before adding, 'A little backward-pointing dorsal fin.'

'Just there,' he continued while still pointing at the place where four pairs of eyes were now focussed most determinedly.

Nothing more happened for five minutes, for fifteen, for twenty-five. There was time to find a book and try to identify the kind of whale. It seemed, from John's description, that a false killer whale, *Pseudorca crassidens,* had come our way, that patch of lighter colouration on the chest being such a distinctive feature.

'Nothing false, I bet, about its teeth,' said someone.

'So how long do they take between each dive?' asked someone else, and our whale provided answer by blowing on the raft's other side where none of us were gazing.

And that was how the evening progressed – a blow from the whale, a belated look from us, another blow, a further lateness, and we all remained enchanted. In time we changed our identification, preferring the rather bigger Bryde's whale which could be twice the length of false killers. We gradually became more skilled at swivelling our heads towards the sudden noise, thereby acquiring increasing glimpses of its great bulk. In truth I did not greatly care what name had been implanted on such an amazing creature, with the astonishment of this fellow mammal being quite sufficient. It was huge. It changed each lungful with, as it were, one breath. And it had to breed as all mammals do, with copulation not easy (without limbs), with underwater birth (also tricky with air-breathing mother and child) and lactation (involving underwater teats for the offspring to find and gain the food). What had been so difficult about life on land that this severe alteration proved preferable? And how extraordinary that it had actually been possible, just as it had been possible for some of the early fishes to leave a life in water and live a life on land.

Our whale stayed with us for some twenty hours. John, yes John, was the only individual to see it swim right underneath our raft, from the stern towards the front without touching anything en route. The snortings were as magical as the animal itself. In fact the whole experience was so very astonishing. How could we humans have killed any whales – let alone such monstrous numbers – just a little while ago. In the Antarctic season of 1930/31 some 29,000 blue whales were slaughtered, these all specimens of the largest creatures ever to have inhabited our planet. I was alive that year, and no less so in 1953 when my newspaper employers asked me to visit a British whaling ship recently arrived at Bootle, Liverpool, following its hunting season in the southern summer. At that time the world's whaling fleets were permitted to catch and kill 26,000 'units' per year, with each blue whale being a single unit and 2 or 2.5 of the smaller whales adding up to a single unit. The ship I visited, the *Abraham Larsen* (of 22,974 tons), had done well, although not as well as had been hoped by its officers and crew – with each man receiving a share of the profits, as with prize money in Napoleonic times. Nevertheless I concluded my article blandly with the horrendous killing total that had been achieved.

'In short, the useful products of 2,438 whales are being unshipped before the factory ship that dealt with them goes to Norway for the five months' summer recess.'

Two thousand, four hundred and thirty-eight whales! All for the perfume trade, the pet-food business, candle manufacture and several other products which surely could be created without slaughtering the greatest animals of all. *Abraham Larsen's* formidable total only added up to some 1,500 units being caught and killed, leaving 24,500 for other ships and other nationalities. A greater wonder is that whales were not extinguished totally, as had earlier been achieved with the dodo, the great auk, the passenger pigeon and so many others in less-enlightened times. We on *Antiki* were rejoicing at seeing just one whale, or half-seeing, or catching the merest glimpse of that little dorsal fin, usually the last bit to be observed. Some species may 'display curiosity and approach boats', stated one of our reference books. Indeed they may and we were truly grateful for hour after hour until, with its curiosity no doubt satisfied, 'our' whale went somewhere else, leaving a great gap in our lives.

I wondered why it was necessary, or advantageous, to be so big. I also wondered about size in general. Many of the dinosaurs were not just big; they were colossal. Today's elephants are, of course, sizeable but the ancient herbivore named diplodocus was eighty feet from its nose to its other end. Had humans been around at the time they could have walked, without stooping, between the legs of this formidable creature. And as for Tyrannosaurus rex, the carnivore so beloved by children in particular, that was *several times* a human's height. We can admire their fossilized remains in large museums but can we truly comprehend that colossal size? I think not. We gasp at elephants but, had we shared the planet with those Jurassic reptiles, I have no idea how we might have behaved. As for 'our' whale, I just said 'Gosh' over and over again. So much for being an articulate human being. Gosh was the best that I could do.

Whale numbers are now increasing, but so little is still known about these formidable creatures. Do they continue to grow as the years pass by? How old are the caught individuals? At what age do they begin breeding and how long is their gestation? The books told us that blue whales can reach 200 tons, and also that – however much they favour cooler water – a blue whale colony lives in tropical waters off Sri Lanka. Apparently bowheads can hold their breath for ninety minutes and certain whales live longer than any other animal, even the giant tortoises. Some whales in cold climates possess fifty tons of blubber with half their body weight being fat, and penis length with right whales sometimes reaching nine feet – which surely has to be a maximum for this most positive form of masculinity.

From the sublime to the other end of the underwater scale, we also examined plankton. Plymouth Marine Laboratory had loaned the necessary equipment, and this we diligently used to capture samples on different days and at different water levels. Anyone who thinks that sea water is just sea water must think again. It is a total nursery of living forms. All the bony fishes start their lives among the plankton, having begun as fertilized eggs. Huge numbers of crustaceans, such as amphipods and copepods, remain as plankton throughout their lives. The minute medusas of jellyfish are initially invisible to human eyes, but gradually grow to be one millimetre in size, and then far bigger or even huge, like those with tendrils hanging below for twenty feet or so. There were hydroids among our catch, the other coelenterates that are basically stomachs in which food is impelled before being rejected when its nutrition has been absorbed. In among them were minute worms which, as with everything else among the plankton, had started life as something smaller still.

Unfortunately – and it was a very great sorrow – all these living and generally mobile forms tended to die quite quickly when their water warmed to our cabin's temperature. When dead they became less visible and even seemed to vanish or become mere blobs instead of the living assortment they had behaved so energetically just moments earlier. (Memo to self:

84

arrange for some refrigeration on any future rafting.) Our most amazing catch, looking initially like a fish with fan-like fins, proved to be a glaucus and therefore one of the nudibranchia. These are molluscs without any protective shells, and the species we encountered cleverly steals the stinging – and formidable – cells of the Portuguese man-of-war, thus arming itself against attack, as when humans capture an enemy's guns and turn them round to fire at their former owners.

I had thought of eating plankton, thus mimicking the baleen whales which thrive this way, but the quantities we caught, however absorbing, would have been the slenderest of appetizers and I, if restricted to this food, would have shrunk in size very speedily. Blue whales keep their massive bulk, and steadily increase it, by favouring the euphausiids that flourish in their many million tons, notably by Antarctica. These shrimp-like creatures are some three inches long, and therefore hugely better for assuaging appetite than the one millimetre (or smaller) objects which we collected further north, but whales down south must gather many tens of thousands to make a meal, particularly as they often refrain from eating for many months thereafter. Our plankton hauls steadfastly informed us of the biological soup, the immense variety of living things that so surrounded us. We used this water in which – already conveniently salted – we cooked our food, and in which we also washed our clothes before giving them clean – and salt-free – rinsing from our piped supply, but we never forgot its massive role in providing such a perfect medium for so much sea life to begin. Scoop up even a handful, and there are bound to be eggs and larvae and youngsters and innumerable other forms, all living their little lives while they search for food and – if possible – escape being food for others.

A good friend, fellow author and global traveller named Douglas Botting once had the temerity to rewrite and add some opening words for the Book of Genesis. He had taken note of creation in general, of days being separated from nights, and of the living things that creepeth upon the Earth, fly in the air or swim in the sea. Therefore he considered it entirely reasonable, following such a deal of labour, that a Creator should rest upon the seventh day. It was the eighth day that concerned my friend and which, in his opinion, needed elaboration, such as some instruction. He therefore suggested that all these fowls, these beasts, these things that swam, that flew and crept should be given advice now that they had been created. This, in my friend's eyes, was quite straightforward, namely 'Start eating one another'. There was no need to recommend escape, that desire being built into the creeping crawling forms. Instead there was straightforward exhortation that food for living things could only come from living things. On the ninth day, in my friend's subsequent opinion, every living thing could rest, having taken its fill sufficiently by consuming loads of other living things one day earlier. I think this man had been experiencing a particularly carnivorous evening on television, with baby gazelles no longer seen and photographed than jumped upon by lions and cheetahs, with hyenas joining in the leftovers, with vultures tearing at their share, and so much life being consumed as food by others so relentlessly. In any case his eighth day jurisdiction did seem to hit the mark, whether among plankton or within every other niche, as biologists like to name the myriad places where living things exist – and then die if bigger, faster, stronger or more lethal fellow creatures find them and promptly attack them as handy nourishment.

On our raft David did almost all the plankton catching before transferring the captures into formalin. He did not choose to look at the collected creatures, neither did Andy nor John. It seemed, as our journeying progressed, as if we were each retreating inwardly, with crowding and proximity not the problem I had foreseen but, instead, isolationism. I had imagined otherwise and wondered if we would each become even more withdrawn as the journey lasted. David, more than anyone else, was often deaf to the outside world, his ears plugged into some machine giving him music, or talk, or whatever else he fancied. Andy often stalked about the raft in solitary fashion, hoping to get some perfect picture that had so far eluded both him and his amazing camera. John read book after book, always reaching its final pages. And I, tediously dissimilar to the other three, did not talk to myself but, as near as dammit did so, and often wondered if some internal thoughts had actually expressed themselves out loud. Laughter was a rarity but so was conviviality. At least that was how I summed up our situation when, so very much alone, we four became yet lonelier.

'How are you all getting on together?' was often asked via emails.

'Very well,' we generally answered, this being shorthand for the four of us becoming increasingly isolated.

Of course we were separate individuals, as are identical twins (who are never identical – ask their mothers), as are extremely close-knit partners (who can fall to pieces should one die), and as are all of us who live and die alone, but something even lonelier seemed to be occurring upon our raft. There was chat but this was never – as I heard it – of the revealing kind, as I had thought might happen. One trouble, one escape-valve, was communication with the outside world. Almost from the start there were near-daily messages from the three wives sending best wishes and intimacies to the three married men onboard. We had two computers but only one fully connected and in service – with the other being spare. Therefore, as we all knew the single password (which was Raft!), we had to read the outgoing and incoming words so relentlessly produced. These were not exactly riveting to the other three of us, and were soon neglected, but they consumed much time for everyone onboard. I think – I know – we would have been more of an assembly had there been no such intrusion. However, as it could not be cancelled, we had to live with it which was, I think, a shame.

On the plus side I could dwell upon my own thoughts and I certainly wondered, for example, about pollution of the Atlantic. This thought tended to surface as and when we jettisoned bottles, tins, paper and other legitimate bits and pieces. The oceans have so long been a dumping ground – for everything. It was therefore good when international legislation took note of the fact that great harm was being done by jettisoning, by exhibiting complete disregard for the purity involved in our surrounding seas. In 1970, while surveying every beach around the British mainland, I and my nine companions on that foray had been appalled by the ease with which we picked up plastic gunk (so called) from the precious playground so favoured for holidays in particular. We could not measure the radioactivity, but were appalled when learning – from Sellafield, for example – of the quantities dumped offshore, just as sewage was often dumped, and condoms, and seemingly everything no longer required on land. Thor Heyerdahl had expressed dismay when meeting surface oil while his reed-boats were taking him, and others, across the north Atlantic but we saw nothing of the sort. Two pieces of polystyrene were all we ever witnessed – and captured – from our lower vantage point. It was therefore good to learn that recent law was undoubtedly having an effect – and long may it do so.

We were still steering west at 270 degrees, more or less. We were still near enough to the nineteenth parallel, but David was steadily stepping up his anxiety. One day, and most dramatically following a lengthy call from home, he suddenly announced a piece of news already known to us:

'It looks as if I'll be losing both my wife and my job.'

We all heard him – of course we did – but there was nothing much the other three of us could say. I know I said nothing, and I think the other two were also quiet. As ever I resented the ship-to-shore communication but it could not be denied. It seemed to be steadily sniping at my wish to reach Eleuthera. Why should a wife and a job be combining to erode my long-held desire? Get another wife, I muttered to myself. Find another job. Push David overboard or somehow shut him up.

What he was wanting, even if not detailed, was an earlier landing than Eleuthera. The Bahamas were a great deal further than, for example, the Leeward Islands. At our speed it would take another four weeks or so even to reach these nearest places but we had solemnly determined back at VGR (over all that beer) that my wish should be obeyed. There had been no suggestion or even mention of an alternative destination. Travelling to the Bahamas would certainly add four additional weeks but their land was where I wished to go and that had been agreed. There had been no talk of wives or employment and a possible curtailment of our trip. On the other hand, as I knew full well, the nearest islands – such as the Leewards – were a mere twenty minutes flying time from David's home, where wife and work existed.

My enthusiasm for landing at Eleuthera in the Bahamas went very deep. I had never forgotten the tale of the two lifeboat survivors in 1940. During my lengthy time as a freelance writer I had often worked for the BBC and, in the early 1990s it had been suggested that I should tell a set of stories which, in their different ways, had lodged themselves unforgettably within my head. Such as Douglas Mawson's terrifying time with Antarctic crevasses, and such as the lifeboat saga. It was then over half a century since those two merchant seamen had experienced their ordeal – but the horror was none the worse for that. Anyway, I told it for the regulation fifteen minutes and that I thought was that, save for a man named Denny subsequently asking for a copy of the script. The First Officer in the boat had also been so named and, in sending off the pages, I asked if – by any chance – the two of them were related.

'He was my brother,' came the blunt reply.

It had not crossed my mind that the transmitted talk, scattered so liberally from Broadcasting House, might actually encounter someone for whom that particular and ancient tragedy of the war was, in its way, a more critical event than the major wartime happenings, such as Dunkirk, El Alamein and D-Day. This brother then suggested that he and I should meet at the forthcoming Remembrance Day service held near Tower Bridge at the Merchant Navy memorial. I had not known beforehand that royal and political events at the Cenotaph on 11 November seem to largely disregard the civilian fleet which transported half of Britain's food, all its petrol, every American and great quantities of military hardware from overseas. Its sailors were not of the armed services (or in uniform) but a greater proportion of them had died than those serving in the Army, Navy or Air Force.

In any case I soon met Desmond Denny and we two also met Ted Milburn, a merchant seaman whose Chief Engineer father had died on the *Anglo-Saxon*, the ship whose sinking had led to the lifeboat story. After singing 'for those in peril on the sea', and watching numerous wreaths placed most reverently, we repaired – as the saying goes – to a nearby pub where we talked and talked. Eventually, and before going our separate ways, the two of them came to a conclusion.

'We must get that boat back.'

Oh yes, I thought; a great deal easier said than done. The boat had been eleven years old at the time of the *Anglo-Saxon*'s sinking, and its unprotected wooden construction had then been subjected to seventy days in tropical waters. As for events since October 1940 I had no idea what might have happened, but imagined some resident Bahamian making use of the boat until, after several decades, the thing was no longer functional. From the launching in 1929 to the 1990s was a reasonable span for any clinker-built construction, and I was not optimistic about its continuing livelihood.

So much for pessimism. The object, as I eventually learned, was safe within an attic belonging to Mystic's Seaport Museum in Connecticut. I therefore asked that organization, having passed this good news to the other two, if this ancient thing could be repatriated. After all, it was a British boat and it had landed on a British island together with two British sailors. The museum's director was immediately helpful and forthcoming but stressed that I would have to find a good home for it in Britain and also contact the family who had donated it to Mystic, thereby gaining official consent for the transfer. I should also arrange for the boat's transport across the broad Atlantic because the museum had no intention of paying for such lengthy voyaging.

These obstacles, most magically, were all overcome. It now rests, I am very happy to report, within London's Imperial War Museum. It is quite their largest object commemorating the service rendered, and the sufferings experienced, by the British Merchant Navy when war had so lethally come its way.

Any visitor to that boat should take particular note of the little notches cut on the port gunwale, as there are twenty-eight of them. There are not seventy, the actual number of days spent sailing and drifting from east to west. Instead that lesser quantity underlines the wretchedness onboard, the lack of care and the sense of hopelessness. To begin with there had been hope, with talk of the Leeward Islands, and notches had been cut. When those four weeks had passed by there had remained no sign of land, and also no food or water. Besides, when in a stupid rage, one man had thrown the axe at another and it had tumbled overboard. It had been the cutting implement, but what the hell! Who now cared about ticking off the passing days? What was the point? What indeed when, without nourishment of any kind and without even shade, you are lying in the bottom of a boat and all hopefulness has gone.

I had no relations on the *Anglo-Saxon*. I did not even have any who had served in the Merchant Navy but that single sinking had involved me deeply since 1942. It was no casual tale told to me one evening. It had inspired thoughts of the Atlantic, first with a Belgian hulk, then by a broadcast; next by the hours, and days, and weeks (and money) I spent seeking the all-too-relevant boat, and finally by its discovery and proper exhibition. My wish to land at the very spot on Eleuthera where the two men had arrived was therefore integral to this sixty-nine year history. It was almost a piece of me. It would be a culmination.

David was looking at a chart.

'I reckon it'll take another month for us to get there from the Leewards,' he said – as if I did not already know – 'and the winds will probably be coming from the north-east while we will be wanting to go north-west.'

I knew that too, but knew of nothing I could say. Instead I watched him roll up the chart and replace it in the rack before we both went our separate ways, in so far as this was possible when living on a raft. I was still eager for Eleuthera. David – as was becoming plainer by the day – had other ideas. Time would tell which of us would have the final say and how this dilemma might be resolved.

8

The Atlantic, of course, has a formidable and quite invisible history of its own. It may look pristine, exhibiting nothing of former happenings, but that is not to deny them. The psalmist had long sung of those 'that go down to the sea in ships, that do business in great waters', and it was upon the greatness which we sailed. The waves around us were not of course the same as in earlier days, but their appearance was as identical to all their predecessors as could be. It was therefore easy to think of earlier times, of desperate voyages, of sinkings great and small, and of major battles fought upon that heaving surface which we were getting to know so well. In particular, egged on by the *Anglo-Saxon* story, I remembered the Battle of the Atlantic, the one fought between 1939 and 1945. It was, said Churchill, the conflict which had most worried him during all those worrying years.

Its statistics underline the cause of his concern. Annual losses of Allied merchant ships sunk during those seven years tell the story almost entirely on their own, as they remorselessly increased – and finally lessened – from 47 to 375 to 496 to 1,006 to 285 to 31 to 19. The peak year of 1942 – with almost three ships a day vanishing beneath the waves – was the one culminating in El Alamein and the loss of Stalingrad. People were then daring to say that a tide was on the turn, but that was the fourth year of the war and 1,922 ships had already vanished, these totalling 10 million tons. (The *Anglo-Saxon*'s tonnage, with its forty-one men, was 6,000.) Not only were the ships lost but, of course, their cargo had disappeared as well, whether food for a beleaguered Britain or vital war material. In any case it was haemorrhage of a terrifying kind.

U-boats were the principal villains but it is easy to sympathize with their plight. Being encased within a steel tube was bad enough but hearing the rivets ping when depth charges came too near often presaged a very nasty form of death. To begin with the German crews had what they called the 'happy time', with sinkings relatively easy to achieve, but then came the horrific aftermath with, in total, 80 per cent of the underwater fleet failing to survive. These annual losses, as with ship sinkings, also tell the Atlantic battle story almost entirely on their own, as they ranged in those same seven wartime years from 6 to 18 to 19 to 35 to 150 to 111 to 71. Such destruction meant a total of over 20,000 men truly learning what it felt like to experience death by submarine.

We on our raft were jettisoning tins and bottles overboard – making what we called the Tesco trail – and these were nestling among the remains of 410 U-boats along with 1,922 of their surface victims. The Atlantic's waves may jauntily rise and fall above these carcasses, but the relics are assuredly down there, along with all the other vessels that had had no need of a war to send them to their graves. Even the famous *Mayflower* very nearly added to their number when certain all-important timbers began to separate but – despite the colonists having nothing onboard to help them live a brand-new style of life in a brand-new land – one man had possessed a formidable jack which, oh so fortuitously, had then bound the famous ship together.

I could never sit on our raft's deck without thinking of Atlantic voyaging in general, of the nightmares that had happened, of wartime loss, of peacetime tragedy. At times I became a merchant captain, longing to go faster than the convoy's slowest ship. I was also an ordinary seaman, playing cribbage in some wardroom and caring more about winning a few pence than possible torpedoes blasting the ship to bits. Of course I was also a submariner, keeping a tight hold on myself for fear of panicking and therefore staring stony-faced at nothing in particular. If such thinking could be totalled, I probably spent more time beneath the waves than on the surface in some merchant vessel, the horror of being encased in steel more vividly understood than the terror of wondering whether my ship would be chosen for destruction rather than others astern or ahead of me. A heightened sense of claustrophobia has been with me for a very long time, and most positively since the age of seventeen.

Owing to much earlier error (on my part), with days having ticked by faster than I had realized, it suddenly transpired that only three options were available when my call-up time arrived. I could be sent down a coal mine, I could 'volunteer' for HM Submarines or join the RAF as potential aircrew. British coal mines were then killing roughly one man every day, and wartime underwater craft were achieving something similar, but flying was my choice and I opted, without further hesitation, for taking to the air. This made no sense statistically, in that death by crashing from on high was far more probable, but the horror of confinement put paid to such reality.

'It doesn't matter what you do when flying,' said old hands, 'so long as you don't hit the ground when doing it.'

The word 'phobia' seems to imply an unreasonable attitude. It is 'morbid fear or dread', states a dictionary. I consider it entirely comprehensible; so too the form of anxiety when standing by a cliff or with half a mile of rock above your head. When sitting on the raft I commiserated more with those experiencing, or fearful of, an underwater death than the

Allied seamen who suffered their ending in some kind of open air, even if this was cruelly mixed with flame or oil or detonation. Of course it was a nasty war, whichever way one looked at it, but underwater death seemed the worst option by far.

On the raft, with thoughts arriving so casually and under less control than was normal, I realized that most of the participants of that wartime fight were probably dead by the time *Antiki* drifted across the graveyard of their less fortunate compatriots. The survivors would have been within their late eighties, and therefore likely to have succumbed, not of course to warfare but to the savagery of life. So too Richard Hillary's accomplices who had luckily stayed alive and had read his book, such as fellow pilot 'Stapme' Stapleton, a particularly memorable crony who had died in his sleep at ninety-five. This line of thinking led me, with the eternity of waves failing to call a halt, to pondering my own age and what it meant being eighty-four.

The newspapers had made much play of this fact. 'Raft of the Summer Wine' headlined one of them. 'Grand-dad goes to Sea' wrote another, as if there was something laudable or strange about that parental title. Yes, I was a generation older than the members of my crew but – however contrary this may seem – I did not feel that way. In any case how should one feel when aged eighty-four? The bells of hell may be ting-a-ling-a-linging somewhat louder, but life – at least for a few more years – is not so much possible as probable, with the actuarial tables telling so. On the raft I was not confronting my own mortality, as someone said, but confronting a further spell of life – as were the others. Thus it has ever been for all of us, and will forever be, until white-coated individuals around one's bed nod too sagely and perhaps too blatantly about one's bodily status. Until that day dawns – or sets – I will carry on, much like everyone else, assuming that lunch will follow breakfast and a sunrise will be partnered by a sunset at the other end of the day.

Of course personal haste in getting about has diminished, as has general ability and a great deal more; but so what!

'Am I dying or is it my birthday?' demanded eighty-four-year-old firebrand Nancy Astor following a stroke, when visited by her youngest son.

'A bit of both, Mum,' he replied.

Haste and ability have also lessened by age sixty-four, or forty-four, or even lower if the truth be known. Sports commentator David Coleman often spoke, and relentlessly, of athletes being 'over the hill' or 'still at it, quite incredibly' when microscopically aged, perhaps twenty-four if they are swimmers or younger still if they are athletes who are good with parallel bars. I have long ceased to run for a bus, climb stairs two at a time or offer to lift a load. I now wear a hearing aid, which I boxed every night on the raft to be certain of its good service on each following day. But it never surprises me that I cannot remember names – I found such titles quite difficult even when young and am not dismayed that the inability still thrives.

Andy, the doctor of our crew, probably felt a touch concerned by my presence on the raft, as there undoubtedly exists a fat file of medical mayhem relating to my past, but this did not seem to trouble him (or perhaps, like many a medic, he kept his thoughts concealed). On only two occasions did he measure my blood pressure and then time my pulse, partly, I think, to show he possessed a sphygmomanometer, as the inflating things are curiously called. Presumably the odds were against me in particular should something choose to strike, but he and the other two were near their sixties and there were three of them. A betting man might consider that the onboard trio formed a greater hazard than the older singleton which was me, but no one ever raised the topic and the thousand

97

dollars-worth of medication brought with us kept its value . . . almost to the end. When, one day, that Canadian medical man offered to educate me about the shower procedure it was not my health or welfare, I believe, which had prompted him but sensitivity to aroma, by then probably one stage up (or is it down?) from easily detectable.

As for the possibility of death, I have always found living to be a little strange. So much is going on without, as it were, one's personal involvement. The heart still pumps, having begun to do so a mere twenty-five days post-conception. In most of life every blood corpuscle reaches the heart again just one minute since its previous visit. Fantastic and amazing! One's body goes to sleep and then becomes awake without any of our say-so in the matter. In fact the bodies which are us do best without interruption or interrogation. If anyone starts to think about going down the stairs they probably fall – or at least stumble. The body does very nicely on its own, whether its owner is aged one or two or rather more. If I look into a mirror nowadays I do realize there has been great change. The sight is not the Me that I see in all those earlier photographs lying within albums, not by a very long chalk, however long that chalk may be. In short there is nothing peculiar about being eighty-four whatever the headline writers say. One day, of course, my years will cease increasing – we all know that however old we are – but we do not know in advance (most thankfully) when that day will dawn, whether at eighty-four, or sixty-one, fifty-eight or fifty-seven. I certainly knew of an elderly woman who said 'Bugger' whenever waking from her sleep. She wished to die but relentlessly went on living. Miles Kington, the excellent comic writer, was told he had little life left to live:

'So who will tell the dog?' he mused, as originally as ever.

A raft ought to be a place, with so much time to spare, for discussing – at great length – many topics which have to be curtailed in ordinary life when something interrupts, the phone rings or a person arrives. No such person was coming our way in mid-Atlantic, but talk of the deeper kind never came to pass. I remember hearing of two philosophy under-graduates who had encountered a particular signpost when motoring in France. One of its arms had pointed to 'Dijon' and the other to 'Toutes Directions'. The two men felt this conundrum needed thought; so they stopped the car, bought a bottle and revelled in the kind of talk their age and special-ity welcomed, if given half a chance.

'Do realize that, behind all the artificial tinsel in the world, there lies the real tinsel,' one of them had memorably said that day to earn a happy laugh.

On our raft it became possible to feel, not so much crowded by the others, as lonely in their company. However, everything changed before the night-time shift. Post-supper entertain-ment, apart from card-playing, often involved listening to old-time favourites on a golf-ball-sized transmitter – *Hancock's Half Hour, Fawlty Towers, Yes Minister*. But occasionally and as an alternative, there was argument and discussion – did the equinox truly mean that everywhere on Earth during two days of each year experienced light and dark in equal measure? Very stupid things were said, but there was never rancour. We all seemed keenest on keeping peace than winning wars with words. The raft was just too small for such belligerence.

Nevertheless, despite the silences which occurred, and despite one's own thoughts about various statements which had been made, the cabin was a pleasing place to be when each day was near its end. Our hut possessed chocolate, always welcome, along with a homely kind of warmth. It contained the computer, the GPS, the other instruments and a goodly number of books. My spell of duty outside, the 9.30 p.m. to midnight watch, always put an end to such conviviality as had existed and I regretted that conclusion. It was therefore with a feeling of weariness that I put on the compulsory safety harness plus some extra clothing, found a torch, arranged a few nibbles if so inclined, and levered my legs into an upright position before, Oates-like in the Antarctic, bidding the others farewell and departing. The cabin's interior, for all its limitations as a living space, did seem a better place to be.

This feeling changed the instant I stepped beyond that cabin's door. As like as not all the stars were there, positioned just as they had been one day earlier. The night was always brighter than expected, with the stars each adding their mite of illumination to that outside world. The fact of their arrival was a form of revelation. The single light bulb that is our sun banishes them so completely that it is almost possible to believe they have gone elsewhere during the brighter time of day. Instead of one great shining – too powerful for actual inspection – there is a multitude, an astonishing assemblage, an entire sky-full of lesser lights which are infinitely more appealing. As if aware of such a change, the outside air has a velvety and softer feel than is ever known each day. It is gentler, unless there is a gale, and is more pleasing than the daytime stuff we breathe. It too reflects the fact that night-time is not just different but actually superior to the previous dozen hours. For that and other reasons, such as one's eyes gradually improving their visual ability as the initial minutes pass, the 2.5 lengthy hours I had been contemplating, the 150 minutes of external tedium, the period I had to suffer before my replacement could be woken, suddenly altered from being a definite duty to a major joy. Perhaps I could let my successor sleep a little longer, and then deceitfully regret my carelessness having been selfishly indulgent with the night-time spectacle.

Everything was better still when there was a moon, or rather when this single natural satellite put in an appearance during one's time outside. How inferior our time on Earth would be if there was not this supreme neighbour busily encircling us.

It is not only so bright when opposite the sun, and when we say the thing is full, but is particularly enchanting when it is crescent, and we say that it is new. While we were on our trip the moon happened to reach the nearest point to Earth that it ever achieves during each twenty-year cycle, then being only 230,000 miles away from us rather than the 250,000 when at its furthest point. I cannot say that it looked brighter when so near because each full moon always takes me – and doubtless others – by surprise, looking brighter and bigger than it has ever done before.

We city dwellers do our very worst to banish night-time virtues. We have street lamps to light us on our way and complain if they let us stumble by being insufficiently illuminating. Only in the countryside can we experience real darkness but, even then, we do not choose to admire that scene for 150 minutes. Instead, as like as not, we hurry indoors, switch on lights and have nothing more to do with night. As for the moon, it always takes us by surprise, suddenly appearing through the windscreen or suddenly appearing anywhere. We note that it is full or halfway there, and then worry that we do not know if its visible bulk is apparently growing or actually diminishing. I treasured a letter sent to my newspaper which chastised the American astronauts for travelling to this satellite when it was only half-exposed.

'Why not wait until it is full,' she wrote, 'as the target will then be bigger.'

When a ship is sailing to the horizon we watch it gradually disappear, and tend to assume mere distance is getting in the way. Of course it is the roundness of the Earth and, hugely belatedly when upon the raft, I learned of the dome of water separating east from west, and the continent of Africa from everything American. With pen and paper I drew such a dome, with the 3,000 miles we were travelling being a neat one-eighth of Earth's circumference. To draw a straight line from our starting point, the lovely harbour of Valle Gran Rey, to some sort of destination within the West Indies shows that direct streak passing through rock (or whatever is down there) rather than following the curve that we surface dwellers actually follow when journeying from east to west. With trigonometry – never a favourite subject – coming to my aid, and with sines and tans involved, I came to the conclusion that, at our mid-way point, we would be 410 miles *above* that straight line passing so directly from starting east to ending west. I found this fact amazing. The Atlantic *is* a dome. It is not flat, and neither is the modest village pond if measured carefully. If our planet did not have 78 per cent of its surface covered by water but 100 per cent – after all the mountains have tumbled into the sea – the oceans would not be dome-shaped but quite spherical. Gravity would then hold all the water in place, just as it holds the oceans nowadays. This may not be the greatest revelation ever to hit a human being, but I had never thought of it either when on land or zapping at 600 miles an hour when stiffly cramped within an aeroplane.

Gravity is such an odd force – at least I find it so. It is hard to comprehend that our bulk, the planet on which we stand, is keeping that moon in place. I also might as well confess that the same goes for Earth itself. We are held in place by the sun, taking one year to make each circumnavigation, and that – I find – is equally incomprehensible. This inability will, no doubt, stay with me for the remainder of my days. Even drop-ping a stone is extraordinary, as it happens instantaneously and I envy all those humans untroubled by that event. There is much to be said for ignorance, when staring at the sky and worrying about the basic laws which hold everything in place.

There is also a great deal to be said for listening to sounds when on the night-time shift. Every plop, each splash and every unknown noise becomes that more intriguing when arriving from a pitch-black sea. As for a whale's snort, that is hugely more extraordinary when coming, always so unexpectedly, from the nothingness out there. It is even frightening, with its distance from the raft so utterly unknown. It is a Jurassic reptile of a sound, an invasion of one's space, a noise that does its awesome best to bring blood flow to a halt. As with children half-longing to be terrified, I goose-pimpled at the sound before feeling glad at having heard it – and even privileged. Noises were so much better for surfacing at night. By sleeping for eight hours or so, and being in our manmade burrows for such a length of time, we almost forget that half the day is night. For many creatures the darker point is far and away the more important. It is when they come alive, to hunt or be hunted, to chase or be chased, and only when daylight arrives do they then settle down for sleep. When living within the Serengeti reserve in Tanganyika, I loved to hear the lion's gasping form of roar arriving from just beyond the canvas of my tent.

'It's all happening out there,' I once said, as if this were a discovery, but the fact was true enough.

Clouds were also much improved at night when, fluffier and lighter than their daytime brethren, they added to the sky. When the sun is shining brightly they can be seen as spoilsports by preventing all that radiating splendour from travelling to the ground. At night they are enchanting extras, not like the moon or even stars, but as a further and exciting ingredient adding to the mix. In fact, to generalize in a manner I never thought back home, the Atlantic night – for countless reasons – did form the better time of day, and it was always easy then to wish for even more of it.

'Oh sorry,' I would therefore say to my replacement, 'I hadn't realized it was that late.'

9

John Russell, the last man to join the crew (and also the last to arrive at Valle Gran Rey), did not – on paper – seem the sort of person who might hurry to embark upon an Atlantic Raft. He had been a solicitor for some four decades and had been senior partner for three of them. He lived near Oxford, commuted daily to his desk in Stroud and was aged sixty-one. He had chosen Stroud because his then wife, Angie, was a multi-lingual stewardess with British Airways and she wished to be within easy reach of Heathrow without living near London. The M4's directness, with good countryside nearby along with country living, helped to make a satisfactory compromise. She liked the long-haul flying which came her way, and saw the world via 707s, VC10s and even the supremely shapely Concorde.

Following their marriage in 1976 they created three children, these born in 1980, 1982 and 1986. Their house was good, their garden was large, they had two incomes, and donkeys were soon added to the mix. Everything, or so it would seem, was perfect – until divorce arrived in the later 1990s. Angie was first to remarry while John, without a partner in sight, lived in various ancient houses and stuck to his job in Stroud. Eventually he encountered Sue, married her and also welcomed her young daughter, the product of a previous relationship. He still gets on well with his children, his former wife, his new stepchild, and he moved into Sue's small and happy house in a village near Oxford. It could be easy to presume that this material does not make him a likely volunteer for rafting from east to west across the broad Atlantic, but presumptions can be wrong.

On the journey I speedily learned that, when he leaves his office chair, he often travels well away from it. In short he skis, sails, explores canyons, paddles canoes and does long-distance walking. He also swims a lot, with him and Sue demonstrating their form of synchronous diving when each decided on bathing from the quayside where *Antiki* was first moored. He also knew beforehand about the raft venture (by clever work on the Internet) which helps to explain why the call from David received such a swift response. Not only did the two of them know each other, but John's decision had already been made. Given half a chance he would volunteer to join the raft – and so he did, within seconds of the call.

Dr Andrew Bainbridge seemed much more probable as another volunteer. Brought up in Harrogate, and having qualified at Liverpool, his move to western Canada was plainly out of the ordinary. Most Yorkshire men like their place of birth too much to think of moving elsewhere, but Andy had certainly moved away and was therefore a likelier candidate than most for embarking upon a raft. The year 1976 had been of major importance for him, particularly its seventh month. On 4 July he had celebrated his twenty-second birthday, on the 10th he had graduated as a doctor and on the 17th he had been married to Diana at Grasmere in England's Lake District.

The two of them liked the idea of emigrating and good vibrations had come from Canada where a couple of Andy's medical friends had visited as locums. After six years in Harrogate, the only place he really knew, he and his Di thought they were deeply in a rut. Therefore Andy applied for six months' work at Turtleford, Saskatchewan, and that half-year proved inspirational. The young couple liked the feel and look of the enormous country and settled for emigration in 1982. In particular they both welcomed the idea of Alberta, it being so wildly different from Harrogate by possessing massive mountains and great opportunities for skiing. (Rain and population pressure were two further reasons for leaving England's shores.)

Andy found work, and so did Di as a substitute teacher. Through Di's school, Andy met a woman named Beryl and the plot then thickened, as they say, with Beryl and Andy growing ever closer. Beryl had two children but, otherwise, was on her own. Di eventually moved to British Columbia and Andy married Beryl in 1991, having bought their property two years earlier, the place that was to be their home for twenty years. Therefore ripe material for a raft trip? It might not seem so, with the leap from Yorkshire so satisfactorily accomplished, but Beryl liked travelling, particularly away from the Canadian winter. She had a small van and he once took a year off work, enabling them to drive to Florida. In the West Indies, assisted by old schoolmate David (already resident in the Virgin Islands), they sailed a lot and this became a habit in later years, particularly after buying their own 36.5-foot ketch. Encouraged by the fact that Canada permits its citizens to build their own houses, even if short of experience or credentials, Andy and Beryl took on this task and moved into their new dwelling in 2002. Within its few surrounding acres they could look after a group of llamas – these originally acquired to serve as pack animals for long-distance hiking among the hills, but no one had asked the animals whether this idea appealed to them. Now they are just known as pets. Whether all this extra material made the doctor more ripe for rafting would have been hard to tell – as I only learned it after he had accepted – but I do know it took him two whole weeks before saying 'Yes'. He is, he says, a cautious type. His Beryl, he admits, is much more impulsive. One curious certainty was that he could take lengthy time off work, a fact which became more relevant as our trip progressed.

As for David Hildred, the fan and recruiter of Andy and John, his life seemed tailor-made for such a venture. Whether inspired to do so by my own life, and that ballooning book's purchase when he was aged thirteen, was a moot point – about as moot as points can be – but the fact is that he did travel a lot, did find employment up and down the globe, and forever found the need for money to be an irritating inconvenience. When I asked him for details about his peregrinations he gave me twenty-seven pages of handwritten material. From these I learned that he had been a sickly child – bronchitis, asthma, hay fever – and was also insecure about life in general. The arrival of puberty seems to have set him to rights medically and also, to some extent, emotionally. A schoolmaster had recommended civil engineering as a profession, partly because it could readily lead to money and Dave was an outstanding 'hands-on kind of person'. University, as he wrote, was 'great', partly for folk music, for fencing and judo 'and there were always girls'. His first adventure was by Land Rover to the Arctic in northern Norway. That group of travellers thought themselves 'intrepid'.

With training completed he took a job in central Saudi Arabia, and worked for six months before visa problems took him to experience sniper fire in war-torn Beirut. He then 'fell in love with Kenya' and met a girl named Jane before taking a 'gap year' (from what?) to visit South and Central America, this ending with a dugout canoe and 500 miles down the Amazon. Names and words like Galapagos, yacht chartering, Mexico and reed boats speckled his many pages before he 'lands a job' at Bandar Abbas in southern Iran and different words are used – house arrest, revolution, Marsh Arabs, evacuation to Bahrain, building a chicken abattoir and escaping via desert to Jordan. Next he was building his own yacht, falling in love (again) and hurrying to Libya to gain more cash before spending much of it in touring Europe. 'We' explored the Mediterranean in 1986, crossed the Atlantic in 1987, toured the West Indies in 1988, travelled 16,000 miles in the USA and Canada before joining some hot-air balloonists in New Mexico and returning to the Caribbean to build up funds, those in his pocket having 'rather dwindled' with all his travelling. Soon his companion also vanished, partly because she wanted a child. In 1995 she plus a daughter then returned to England. So David took a year off (again from what?) to visit the Far East and Fiji before driving a van around Australia and a car around New Zealand.

It was in 1998 that he met a former acquaintance named Trish (she choosing to be so called after resenting her given name). Her companion and partner had recently been killed in a motorcycle accident and soon 'love happened'. Dave was still getting over his 'fear of betrayal and commitment' but in 2005 the two of them married, both for the very first time. The 'decider', wrote Dave, was the love and care she gave him for six months after a serious fall that 'nearly cost him his life'. They celebrated by going round the world with an 'extended honeymoon' in Europe.

I do not know how other people collect their raft companions but David's CV, with so much travelling and so much experience gained, did place him in a special category. His uncertainties still existed, along with a desire to prove himself worthy, but there was Trish as extra backbone. One American magazine, in writing about our venture, carelessly omitted David's name.

'But you have left out the raft's most important person,' responded Trish almost instantly. 'I should know because I'm his wife.'

Her comment was not welcomed everywhere but did show that love and care were uppermost, even if diplomacy was lower down the list. Her phone calls to him when voyaging, as his to her, did not always seem to end satisfactorily to those of us afloat, and I certainly longed for them to cease. Why could they not resemble the communications between John and Sue or Andy and Beryl? These always brought onboard joy, however much Beryl's were often belligerently anti-snow and Sue's told of her busy life seeing so many kinds of people. (She was not letting the absence of a husband cause inactivity or loneliness. 'I don't do loneliness,' she had said before the start.) Plainly, as I steadily realized, there was more to living on a raft (with all its secrets and sensitive discoveries) than being lonely in a crowd, welcoming the nights more than the days, knowing no other face would come our way for many weeks and living out a long-held dream. Ah well, perhaps we will play cards that evening and feel free to denounce others as shit-faced turds, or rather worse, by their playing of a winning hand. Crud! Loathsome nerd! Scum of the lowest order – whatever that may be. Puerile, but fun, and it always let off steam.

There was also myself as fourth member of this assembly. The others assuredly picked up facts about my earlier days, and certainly learned that I was twice married (1956, 1984), twice divorced (1983, 2008) and had cared for five children, two of them adopted, during all that complicated time. My first child had arrived in 1963 and the last in 1986 when I had just touched sixty. There had been employment, with the *Manchester Guardian, Drum* (in Africa) and the *Daily Telegraph* but this had been halted at the end of 1963, oddly on the very day that witnessed my first-born's magical appearance. Working on the newspapers had been fun, often exciting and frequently exhausting – particularly in West Africa – but each day's fervour often bore no relation to the next day's equally

109

urgent priorities. I wanted to lengthen my stride a bit, stick to
a subject, and work at it for months or even years. In short I
wanted to write a 'major book', as publishers frequently use
the term, and I also wished to create a hot-air airship, which
no one had ever done, this causing publishers to exhibit much
less enthusiasm.

A new kind of life had therefore started in 1964. It meant
the withdrawal of a monthly cheque – from anyone. It also led
to extreme uncertainty concerning cash in general and to the
hiring of an accountant so that he might spread the taxable
income across leaner times when nothing much arrived or,
sometimes simultaneously, when large amounts had to depart.
Fortunately that first major book, which promptly consumed
four of my freelance lifetime's years, did very well indeed. Less
agreeably the airship, although tremendous fun, never left the
ground. And that, more or less, was how my life proceeded.
Any other freelancer will surely sympathize, knowing that projects, ideas and suggestions are frequently embraced – for
their novelty, their stimulus, their undeniable excitement –
without too much inspection of the pounds and pence they
might entail, either as profit or as loss.

Such freelancing does not stop merely because an age, say
sixty-five, has suddenly arrived. No retirement clock is given,
mingled with merry applause from younger work-mates still
employed; no sizeable pension arrives, which it probably does
in regular employment, even if only a fraction bigger than
nothing whatsoever. All this means, in my opinion, that I was
a likelier candidate than most for initiating, and then pressing
forward, the idea of travelling by raft upon an ocean for a
major length of time. It had been almost twenty years since
that important birthday when many people start their official
rest and hang up their overalls or briefcases, obedient to the
fact that 23,741 days – sixty-five years – have been consumed,
this curious milestone having been initiated, I believe, by

Bismarck to remove difficult and argumentative colleagues from his vicinity, all happy to cease work completely if provided with a (lesser) wage.

Such thinking, and the calculations, are not important during the earliest years of adulthood. On my first expedition, to Persia in 1950, only one of us four was married and there were no children. In any case, being youngsters, we cared little about our past, not mentioning our parents (for heaven's sake!) or our sisters (whatever next?) or our schools. We lived entirely for the present, relishing our great new status as undergraduates. Contrarily the raft's foursome, so curiously recruited, had most of their lives behind them, with those seven marriages, four divorces, eight children and four stepchildren in their wake. Life had been a whole lot simpler when chasing degrees, earning qualifications and striving to grip the first rungs of employment.

I suspect that all youngsters, should they find themselves upon a raft, would care little about its quality, it being right and proper to care little about risk and danger when there is so much more life to lose. Thor Heyerdahl, in his famous book, told how he had observed his fellow Scandinavians, just once or twice, cut small slivers from a balsa log before watching these little bits sink beneath the waves, but they made no mention of their curiosity about the continuing effectiveness of logs. To what extent, for instance, had water penetrated the inner layers and might log buoyancy eventually come to naught? That was not a subject for discussion, not with sharks to be caught by hand, a guitar to be played, radio hams to be contacted around the world, Army K-rations to be consumed and a life to be lived so absolutely different from anything on their homeland, this formerly so powerfully occupied by foreign troops. Raabi Torstein, for example, had informed London daily about the battleship *Tirpitz*, with his German enemies immediately focussing their interest upon the precise location of his transmissions. Who could care about dampening logs following such a frightening form of life?

As for our opinions about our own raft, David was most forthright. One day I said that the deck planks seemed to be spreading, with the gaps between them growing greater. He answered that nothing of the sort was happening, as if accused of terrible malpractice in that area. Andy seemed to hold no concerns about its resilience. If David thought the raft was good that was good enough for him. John was more direct. If it tips over, so he had said, we will all be dead. For him there was none of David's optimism about polyethylene tubes remaining buoyant even when full of water. There was just straightforward acceptance of a possibility – observe the raft move through 180 degrees and life itself would also be overturned.

In all my reading of raft ventures during the six decades since *Kon-Tiki* had set sail I had only encountered one death. There may, of course, have been other voyages which were never publicized, with their vanishings making scant material for publication, but Éric de Bisschop's name – and ending – became well known, if only because his disaster seemed so inevitable almost from the start. In 1958, when aged sixty-two, he had embarked as captain on *Tahiti-Nui II* – which makes one wonder about *Nui I* particularly as *II* was soon in trouble, with one man 'going mad' and then starting to saw the raft apart. Landfall was quickly made in Peru, after the departure from Chile, and the failing raft was strengthened by twelve more balsa logs plus fourteen aluminium water tanks. In theory they were heading for very distant Tahiti but in fact were slowly sinking. One night, which must have been terrifying, the entire construction sank three feet and everyone, most reasonably, moved on to the cabin's roof. By then de Bisschop had handed over authority to a younger man named Brun, with the captain feeling too ill to continue in command.

Brun promptly ordered the construction of *Tahiti-Nui III* from the remains of *II*. This later version possessed two outriggers fashioned from aluminium tanks, and was no doubt more stable than its predecessor, but after 180 days at sea they, most reasonably (as viewed from one's armchair), wanted land again, particularly as food supplies had been exhausted. Moreover, of the 100 gallons of water with them at the start, only fifteen remained when Brun took over. The raft passed seventy miles from Starbuck Island (wherever that is) and they were more hopeful, indeed too hopeful, of meeting Rakahanga, a Starbuck neighbour. They speedily hit one of its outer reefs, causing all five rafters to be thrown into the sea. Four of them surfaced, and then reached shore, but the more elderly de Bisschop failed to do so and his body, when eventually discovered, was found to have a broken neck. The only bright spot in this entirely dismal tale is that some of his friends, aware of the long-felt desperation to reach Tahiti, had had his body resurrected and then reinterred on the famous island which had been his goal.

'You are wanting to die,' so many had told him before his trip began.

We also received talk of this nature in the early days.

'I think you're wanting to end it all,' some friends had stated when shorn of argument.

I suppose this really means that they have no intention of doing such a thing themselves. In which case they can live their lives as they think fit, with all their earnest preoccupations back on land – but at times I did see their point of view. Our raft trip did have its many lows along with its several highs. The first days after departure had involved much misery, making me wonder why I had spent so much time and energy, and worry and money, in achieving such a quantity of discomfort. What was wrong with husbanding a hundred polyanthus in little plastic pots? What was wrong with doing anything that

113

was safely on the land? But then came some total joy, such as a warm evening, a gentle breeze, fine clouds, great contentment and an amazing flurry of flying fish.

A confession is necessary here. On first seeing these creatures I had believed them to be birds because what else flies such distances, and so skilfully, just above the waves? On the other hand what kind of flying bird then disappears, and so protractedly, beneath the surface of the sea? Every kind of small boat venture in our locality tells of fish carelessly ending their flights onboard, thus escaping some predator only to reach the frying pan. I had presumed these creatures had earned their title by gliding a modest distance before falling back, more or less whence they had come. I had not imagined for one instant that their flights often covered several hundred yards. No wonder, therefore, that I had thought them birds. If escape from predation was truly the cause of such aerial endeavour, the jaws below did not merely miss their catch but missed it hugely, perhaps by a quarter of one mile.

Another curiosity was emphasized by their steady blundering into our raft. If they were such skilful aviators surely they could avoid such an all-too-conspicuous structure lying in their path. Either, like some crashing aircraft, they had quite lost rudder control or their vision in the air was no longer so satisfactory, particularly in the dark. At all events there was never a night during our Atlantic crossing when such fishes did not come our way to flap exuberantly (while we tried to find them) and then perish (if our search proved to be in vain).

For some reason – or none at all – I was the principal recipient of flying fish attack. Even when lying on my bunk, this often a favoured spot for me, I had once been hit amidships. To achieve this destination the fish in question had first to leap upwards before flying over our raft's surrounding netting along with fifteen feet of foredeck before gliding through the cabin's narrow doorway, evading the electronics desk and then aiming, kamikaze-like, for the horizontal human body straight ahead which was so peacefully at ease. I must admit I then reacted slowly. Had I suddenly been hit by some book cascading from a shelf? Or several onions escaping from their hanging plastic bag for a spell of liberty? Or – no, it had to be a fish to leave such a fishy smell, along with major slipperiness where it had landed upon my frame, before escaping to the floor. Oaths and grunts from all four of us partnered the flapping of one most misguided animal. Or was it actually guided, somewhat mistakenly, and had actually *aimed* for me?

Our policy, never announced but always followed, was to return all such arrivals whence they had come, if they still – so to speak – had flap within them. My oh-so-personal visitor was eventually discarded seawards – with a tale or two to tell the others? Only the dead were retained, either for eating, or interesting observation or merely for fame by photograph. We thought the reference books inaccurate in drawing the flying fish's wings, these – if stretched – being much more extensive than were ever portrayed. The front and pectoral wings were not narrow protuberances, much like an aircraft's aerofoils, but nearer 90 degrees in their possible spread, resembling some flying machines from the earliest and most hazardous days of aviation. Similarly the rear or pelvic fins were not modestly sized, like an aircraft's elevators, but relatively much larger. As for the fish's body that was more rectangular than the average fishy fuselage, no doubt creating some aerodynamic lift as its owner hurtled through the air for those several hundred yards.

We thought our catch – if that is the word for the self-inflicted haul – was mainly Spotfin flying fish or perhaps the Bandwing variety. Our specimens were never large, being nearer seven inches than the twelve to eighteen mentioned in the books. Perhaps the flying youngsters were proving less able to avoid the oddity of a raft appearing in their patch or maybe the smaller young are more numerous than their older brethren. All sorts of questions arose as we contemplated the corpses – why, for example, are flying fish such a tropical happening? They rarely enter cooler waters. Why is there so much similarity between the species? And why do they have to travel quite so far? Landing onboard small craft is so frequently reported that it is difficult to read any voyage's account without there being mention of these suicidal animals risking the possibility of death by cooker.

The birds that take advantage of these aerial endeavours have to be very quick. Each fish's airspeed is quite considerable and there is – of course – no knowing where their trajectories will begin. It is not like rabbits emerging from their noticeable burrows. Instead it is guessing from an entire ocean where an underwater meal will suddenly become an overwater one. The ever-present dorados did leap upwards on occasion, but never – it would seem – to catch fish flying in quite another element. As for poor old Eric de Bisschop, he never seemed to enjoy this kind (or any other kind) of fun. If he did do so it was never mentioned in his diaries, with such a lack being, for him and his long-suffering crew, a very sorry loss.

10

Infrequently – because they were expensive to acquire – we requested 'grib' sheets which gave weather information. In the main these were not necessary, with the east-west trade winds so very reliable, but forecasts are always good to see and hear, if only for casual interest. Initially I wondered about their mid-Atlantic accuracy. How many other craft were out there, enthusiastic to know what might be involved within the nearby atmosphere? I then surmised – but with what accuracy I do not know – that forecasts may be more reliable concerning mighty oceans. On land there are the awkwardnesses which can so disrupt the forecast story – the little hills, the urban concentrations, the darkened forests, the crops of corn – all of which can disrupt generalities issued by the Met Office. Out at sea there are no such differences. There is just sea, just lots and lots of that. With every grib we downloaded when in the trades, it predicted a continuation of the same, with wind blowing remorselessly from the east which was pushing us further and further towards the west.

It therefore came as some surprise one day when the latest grib showed an area of lower pressure bulging into the anti-cyclone which had been sitting, so very faithfully, to the north of us. This was bad news as it might disrupt our intercontinental passage and might even send us in reverse. And that is precisely what it did. For several days we travelled backwards, seeing – as it were – areas of ocean we had already witnessed. It is so correct that atmospheric depressions are often most depressing to those experiencing them. That was certainly the case with us, and particularly with David. He regarded the downturn – or backward turn – as if some kind of personal attack.

'It's so unfair,' he said.

Robert Falcon Scott had famously written much the same in his polar diary. Bad weather had caused his party major setback which he, of course, resented. We need better luck, he wrote; we certainly deserve it. As for the four of us, busily rafting in our less demanding enterprise, we too were encountering bad luck, a vicissitude which happened to come our way. In fact it was some ten days before we were back where – as it were – we had started from. At least we were then heading west again, and meeting lines of longitude not yet encountered. Things were therefore looking up once more, save that the next new grib sheet showed yet another region of low pressure bulging south, just as its predecessor had done. Therefore more anxiety onboard our craft, and more resentment from sailing master David.

'We don't deserve such ill fortune,' he said, and was (almost) off his food.

This time we only suffered for four days before heading west again. Those on land who were following our route via the Yellowbrick tracking system on their computers could see precisely where and how we had travelled, with fresh information given at six-hourly intervals of our actual position marked for all of them to see. Our antics, said some, were like those of some uncertain worm having second thoughts. Or a human being who was returning, every now and then, to retrieve possessions stupidly left behind. Such modest jesting, received via emails, did not go smoothly with those of us onboard.

'Now we'll be even later,' said David, so personally damaged and affronted – it would seem – by these reverses.

118

It was his anxiety about delay which existed at the nub of his saddened attitude. He had hoped – and had indeed promised his employers – that mid-March would witness his return, or perhaps the final days of March if some serious misadventure had come our way. He realized, following the reversals and our overall lack of haste, that we would not reach even the nearest Leeward Islands until April had begun. As for Eleuthera, the intended and planned destination, that should plainly be forgotten because, in his eyes, it had become irrelevant. We, the foursome, had solemnly declared that the Bahamas would be our goal but that intent was about to be shelved, much like any ambition no longer on the cards.

Mutiny is not a proper word for it; neither is insurrection. Nevertheless there was soon a feeling within the cabin that our planned destination could no longer be countenanced. This arose, at the outset, solely from David. One evening he surfaced from yet another major thirty-minute satellite-telephone call to say again that he would be losing both wife and job if we – if I – persisted with our planned intent to reach the Bahamas. This was no idle statement. It was delivered emotionally, as if tears might be the next item on his agenda. Plainly he had been given a harrowing time via the satellite connection, with it providing the information that both marriage and employment were in jeopardy.

It was now March and he had been away from work and wife since the second half of November the previous year. During much of that time, and certainly during the actual trip, David had never been averse to little probings, these reminding me that Eleuthera lay a considerable distance north-west of the much nearer Leewards, that 900 or so extra miles would present a feast of extra difficulties and that wind direction during the extra passage would be consistently unhelpful. The great trade winds blowing from east to west had, until that time, been our (near) constant partners but, even so, had only caused an average speed (thus far) of 2.1 knots. Fifty miles a day seemed reasonable (to me) as haste, but we had neared eighty on a few occasions, creating disappointment that such speed could not be more frequent as a happening.

'I think we had better have a meeting,' I therefore said; 'Let's have it after supper.'

And so we did. Apart from David stressing, as we had already heard, how his Trish was missing him too much, he also detailed promises made to his employers, of mutual agreement that he would be back in mid-March, having by then consumed his permitted four-month leave of absence. At this time on our Atlantic crossing we were still some 600 miles east of any Caribbean isle. Therefore he would be late whether or not we continued to Eleuthera, with our average speed suggesting almost a dozen – or so – more days of sailing before sighting any land. To meet the Bahamas meant an additional four weeks – or so. It was difficult not to see that David had a point. So too, as the meeting was suddenly informed, did quiet John because he too had made a deal with his employers. As he had only arrived at Valle Gran Rey after Christmas his come-back date was later than David's, but a promised mid-April return certainly could not be met if we persisted in our wish, with *my* wish in particular, to reach the destination we had so solemnly agreed. Our eyes therefore shifted to Andy; what did the quiet man from Canada have to say?

'I'm for the long haul myself,' he eventually drawled, 'but, as there are two of us with strong desire to make landfall earlier, I'll cast my vote with them.'

'That means three against one,' I said, while remembering that I too also had some reason for an earlier landing.

The elderly these days, however much they might dispute their age or resent the fact, consume pills. Not all of us do so, and the quantities do vary, but breakfast for the elderly is often cereal plus pills. Perhaps supper is much the same, save that cereal has been replaced by something else. My actual supply of medication was running low and the store would soon be ended. Would I then fall over, suffer breathlessness, feel heart-side pain or mere nausea? I did not know, but certainly knew of a general dictum that prescribed drugs should not be set aside 'without medical advice'. An earlier landing would therefore be best for all four of us, and this fact made me - happier about the decision which we were making after setting aside my longing for the Bahamas.

'PEOPLE WHO GO ON RAFTS SHOULD NOT HAVE COMMITMENTS' as my elder son emailed to me in capitals for all of us to see, when news of our alteration became more widely known.

Wearily and sadly I therefore took down a gazetteer from our shelves, this packed with information about all the islands lying ahead of us. David – who knew many of the pictured places – was all for Antigua or Barbuda, these both 'great yachting centres'. I abruptly saw no reason why I, virtually sidelined in this business, should not have a casting vote, particularly after my eyes had glimpsed Sint Maarten, also known as St Martin, this island having been given that saint's name – however spelt – by the great Columbus on his second voyage. The place itself was endearingly small, being some seven miles wide and seven miles tall, but the reason for its double title was more intriguing. Back in 1648 it had been decided that France should control the northern half and Holland the lower portion. Amazingly, despite Caribbean island ownership switching again and again in more turbulent times, often with warfare intermingled in all the centuries since then, the French and Dutch were still in charge of their separate portions. The wavering frontier between their halves still wavers, just as it first did 366 years ago. The frontier line is far from straight but its existence and persistence are still as firm as ever. (Allegedly the delegates from each half were happily sloshed when frontier fixing, with the current line neatly indicating that genever and some fine wine had served as refreshment during their seventeenth-century stroll across the island that they shared.)

More to the point, and bearing our rafting needs in mind, the lower and Dutch half possessed many little bays for anchorage, plus part of an enormous lagoon seemingly tailor-made and extremely safe for any vessel without some form of motor. To that piece of colonial Holland we therefore sent a message, together with a precise waypoint at which we would like to receive assistance and some kind of tow. As for *Antiki*'s arrival date, that would be 'either Tuesday or Wednesday of the week after next'. This information was somewhat grandiose, in that rafts are not Swiss trains keeping to arrivals and departures with frightening precision; but, after some six weeks of travelling, we had come to know our raft's abilities, along with our own skills – notably David's – at controlling them. Sint Maarten, as we later heard, promptly took this transmitted forecast with considerable calm, printing in its newspapers that a transatlantic venture by pipe raft would be arriving at a given place by Simpson's Bay during a given pair of days.

That done, and with warm words of welcome coming back from that island we had chosen, we settled down to enjoy the final 600 miles of our transatlantic spree. David still worried – that was his way – but he expressed, and certainly felt, considerable determination to hit that way-point on the button. He lived in the Virgin Islands, such a little distance from Sint Maarten, and a successful arrival, almost on cue, would have this news swiftly circulated in his area. Like all of us, I suppose, he would not be displeased should the information spread – and be accurately reported – that he had arrived *by raft* at the very place he (and we) had chosen some ten days earlier.

Therefore, with most anxieties now well behind us, and our confidence almost overflowing, we each settled down to enjoy the several final days of our Atlantic crossing most determinedly.

11

There were not just waves to watch; there were also birds. Initially we had seen nothing of the sort. Even at our departure point of Valle Gran Rey they had been scarce, with pigeons and seagulls almost the only representatives. This appeared to continue, or maybe, with a broken rudder, difficult sailing, contrary waves and plenty of anxiety in the early days, there was no mental space for even lightweight ornithology, such as taking casual note of anything that flew. In fact John was first to see a bird some three weeks after we had started. And what was it? For none of us had seen its kind earlier in life. The books quickly told us – as did the bird itself – that a shearwater had arrived. It was seemingly cutting through the water, being at times so very low. It was a daredevil of a bird, forever on the edge of immersion and teasing the waves to catch it.

In fact this is how these birds operate. They use the shapes of waves to aid their flight, just as man-made gliders fly by hills to gain the uplift which results from all the contours down below. In fact the shearwaters do so well that they scarcely need to flap their wings. We observers now took particular interest in these birds who, with all their skills, shared our sea. How much time would pass between one flap and the next? Astonishingly, in that it truly astonished us, some five minutes passed by before a wing beat was achieved. Even then the action was not desperate, like a first gasp for air after too long a gap. It was just a flap casually undertaken, much like someone might scratch an ear from time to time as something else to do.

The first and single shearwater was soon joined by others and all were a joy to watch. They were so clever in their flying, whether or not they needed waves. Many a bird on land, like some of the very smallest, hammer away with their wings in breathless fashion, as if any cessation might take them to the ground. Others, such as land-based rooks, work their wings in ponderous fashion, never missing a beat to enjoy a glide. They just know that flying means flapping; it always has and always will. Our shearwaters took no interest in the raft, in that their cavortings were never concentrated in our area, but every now and then they happened to come close, causing our whoops of exultation to be yet greater.

'Seven minutes,' we shouted. 'No flap for all that time.'

What fantastic skill! What a magnificent display! I began to wonder for how long they had been practising. Had they swooped and exhibited their art for those onboard the three famous caravels of 1492? Or had they already been doing so when humans were first learning agriculture or using flint to serve their needs. It is true that birds – of a sort, beginning with archaeopteryx – have had feathers and have flown for over 200 million years. So when did shearwaters first arrive, having learned the trick of gaining lift from waves? When did cuckoos learn the game of proxy incubation or swallows their desire to winter in another hemisphere? Humans could walk, and presumably run, several million years before the present. So what were birds doing then, I pondered, and came to no conclusions, but I never tired of looking at the birds.

As further query, we were seeing the birds towards the end of April. Should they not be nesting about this time in the northern hemisphere? Although species living near the equator are less dogmatic about spring being the time for incubation, their nidification, as Bond phrases it in his famous book *Birds of the West Indies* (yes, Bond, James Bond, whose name Fleming appropriated for his 007), occurs in 'burrows or in rock crevices'. How extraordinary that creatures so intimately connected with the great outdoors, and enthusiastically treating the Atlantic as its living space, using air and water so very cleverly, should then exist within a hole and go underground to incubate and eventually raise the product of a single egg. What an amazing shift in circumstance! From oceanic brilliance to excavated darkness is an extreme form of alteration.

The purpose of their low flying is, of course, to encounter food. This is probably most frequently discovered on – and intermingled with – the clumps of so called sargasso weed. Air bubbles exist within these plants, causing them to float, and animals such as crabs may take up residence and treat the place as home. Shearwaters do fly extremely swiftly and their expertise is therefore tested once again. They first have to see some morsel within the weed and recognize it for what it is before pecking at it successfully in the brief moment before the weed plus occupants have passed by. Sitting on the water is a dangerous activity, with big fish ready to attack. Flying a small distance overhead – and then pouncing swiftly – is an amazing task, something to be accomplished only by a species of tremendous aptitude. Shearwaters employ these skills so wonderfully that we watched them for hours and hours on end. Forget books. Stop daily tasks. Just admire, and be amazed.

Nevertheless, we were a disloyal bunch of onlookers. When the frigate birds arrived we switched our eyes immediately to them. Bond, yes James Bond again, calls them 'the most aerial of oceanic birds'. He adds that the species is also known as man-o'-war bird, hurricane bird, scissors-tail and cobbler. Even their Latin name breaks ranks, as it were, by attaching praise instead of mere description. *Fregata magnificens* is their scientific title, and is fully justified. The bird's wingspan is as great

125

even as that of the albatross and looks supreme. (A digression here may be excusable. Aged seven I gave my first public performance and solemnly stated to assembled parents: 'With my crossbow I shot the ancient mariner.' The subsequent tittering did not help personal morale or self-confidence but, on reflection and bearing in mind all the trouble afflicting that old man, I think my alternative choice of destination for a crossbow's bolt may have been more sensible.)

The frigates generally cruise the ocean some 500 feet above it. From there, and with a slow wing-beat, they survey the scene beneath them in quite a different fashion to the shearwaters who are scooting about, more or less at surface level. In particular the higher birds are waiting for flying fish and the sudden leaps they make from water into air. Not only are these fishy invasions into another element speedily achieved but they do not last for ever. With a sudden plop the aerial venturers then vanish out of sight and the frigates therefore have to waste no time in catching this form of meal. They dislocate their 2.2 metre wings, and drop like a rock from their earlier vantage points. If luck – and skill – are on their side they will catch a fish before it vanishes. If not they must laboriously fly back again, empty-handed as it were, to their former post on high.

For such a bird to consume such a fish, having been successful, is also problematic. The quarry may be quite lengthy, far wider than the frigate's bill is broad, and the best such a bird can do is chew and swallow the bit that it holds most captive; the rest just falls away. This is when the frigate's fighting name becomes so correct. As with the similarly titled naval vessels it is an attacker, grabbing opportunities when they arrive, seeking and destroying. Other frigates, having observed the captured beak-borne fish, wait a while and then pounce when bits of fish start falling past them through the air. This is no casual form of feeding, as with birds pecking at seeds upon the ground. It is a chasing for food, a scouring, and more an act of war than mere hunter-gathering. The catchers of these tumbling bits of fish may also find them difficult to consume totally. So bits are dropped, and these are then snatched, and grabbed, and gobbled by further frigates so that nothing meets the sea. The birds are true predators much like the bigger carnivores. And they are magnificent.

We often had dead flying fish to hand, these having arrived on deck without anyone noticing. We therefore tied string to them and, using a pole as a helpful tool, dangled them overboard, hoping that the frigates flying up above might notice this dangling food. Might notice! Of course they did, and very speedily. It was not a matter of seconds before the birds were at sea level and in our vicinity; it was virtually instantaneous. Some half a dozen feet from our viewing platform of a raft there was a sudden flurry of flapping and then the bait had gone. Bits of fish were soon falling; causing more swooping, more snatching and further aerial expertise. At times like these, we four onboard became more harmonious than was our normal style. With Dave performing the fishing, Andy taking pictures, John telling of the birds positioning and me filming as best I could, we were more a band of brothers than four separate individuals, each coping with their independence as was our normal style. The birds were achieving this better form of unity by their supreme flying skill. Therefore not only did we love their particular style of excellence but we welcomed their happy effect upon our individual selves.

The crew certainly excelled themselves when my eighty-fifth birthday arrived. I declined the offered 'breakfast in bunk', sensing that cornflakes might spill and be an unwelcome extra to an already unwholesome sleeping bag, but I certainly welcomed the cake. I think it had four candles (or fork handles as Ronnie Barker told so admirably) but I know it had the figure eighty-five pricked out in well-sliced apricot. As for its ingredients, all selected by Andy, these were a mishmash of wise and erratic choices. It seemed that Marmite had been added when flavour had been thought inadequate, and I cannot say that the cake gained in consequence, but he applied the evening meal technique of adding flavour after flavour to the birthday offering, with taste after taste squirted, poured, squeezed or gurgled as he alone thought fit. It did last, that cake, well into a second week and the manufacturer deserved more credit than he got. He certainly merited the happy applause we gave when, with champagne being poured at the setting of the sun, I suddenly noticed bubbles drifting past the mast. The cake-maker had purchased a bubble creator at VGR, and I opened my two 'pressies' in a haze of exploding soap. These gifts, carefully wrapped in BacoFoil, were of massive chocolate bars, and were therefore hugely appreciated, along with all the food. I retired to my flake-free bunk that evening in a whirl of appreciation. An eighty-sixth year had been initiated very happily.

As for being in my ninth decade, I think this troubled the others more than the fact troubled me. Whenever some bump or ache had surfaced during earlier days I had tended to assume the worst because, plainly, some cancer had begun. On reaching older and senior years I tended to be equally beset with worry – until the lump or hurt chanced to go away. Come to think of it, if the boils, abscesses and fevers which accompanied my time at school arose in my later years I would be beset with concern. As it was, these distasteful and disfiguring early extras were just thought to be another fact of adolescent life, along with smelly towels, short long trousers, holy socks, 'chaps' on knees (unknown nowadays?), chilblains and near-brushless brushes for one's teeth. The short answer about old age is that the elderly are just as ignorant about their finality as in all their previous years. Moreover, people do die when young, when middle-aged or when elderly. Thank goodness we do not know precisely when such conclusions will occur. Science, one day, may let us know. In which case to hell with science in that advance. I have no wish for it.

One memorable evening, a multi-coloured swallow flew into our cabin. The raft did play temporary host to various fliers, such as roseate terns, pigeons and gulls, but such newcomers tended to rest upon our rigging until they chose to go away. Invading our indoor privacy was therefore a novelty. It was also, we presumed, a new experience for our visitor. It certainly stumbled into almost everything, our fire extinguisher, our row of mugs, our clothing resting on its pegs, and we did likewise in trying to catch this unexpected new arrival. Eventually we were successful and gently, firmly, positively held the catch for all to see. That done, and with the visitor fully photographed, we took the bird outside and released it within the darkness of that night. Back therefore to our meal, and to calm once more, when the swallow reappeared. Being now better aware of our cabin and its contents, the arrival flew more determinedly towards the extinguisher in particular. And there it rested, having found a claw-hold to its liking. We were all flattered by this additional visit and saw no reason for further expulsion. Should the new arrival choose to leave our den, the large entranceway to our quarters was entirely open, the bird itself now knowing this fact as well as we all did. Therefore we left the swallow alone and there it stayed, not for a couple of minutes but for the entirety of that night. In the morning, while we were imbibing what it is that coffee gives, the bird got up – as it were – stretched each wing in turn and then departed through the door. It collected up a partner, who must have also lodged onboard, and the two of them departed to the north. We all felt privileged.

Bird books frequently state that this-or-that species is 'often seen from small boats'. There is a hint here, is there not, that one attracts the other. This may have been so with the swallows, but I think the implication is quite wrong. Birds will not be seen, in general, from 20,000 tonners travelling in straight lines from A to B. Neither will they be seen by – who else? Swimmers? Land-based individuals far from waves and fish? I may be pernickety here, but we in our 'small boat' were seeing birds because we were so well placed to do so. There is no relationship between modest craft and the avian world – unless food is being thrown and that we did not do, save with poles and string. Anyhow, sea birds are 'often seen from rafts' and are a most determined joy.

Given half a chance, such as sitting with a ringside view of aerial antics, everyone is an ornithologist, including those whose upbringing might have determined otherwise. My father was very keen on birds. He could tell, at fifty miles an hour with his car window open, if a chiffchaff – for example – was giving voice not too far away. The flip side of this enthusiasm was his habit of using his varied offspring when they were too young to disobey.

'Here are field glasses; just watch that bush and let me know if anything happens; I'll bring you lunch in an hour or two.'

Or I would have to ascend a tree, put my hand into a hole, and describe what I could feel – or could feel me. Worst of all was being tied with rope and made to descend those cliffs that are not proper cliffs. Instead they are land that gradually grows steeper until it is actually vertical. Would I shout back what I saw – yes, just along that ledge – and disregard the angry bird whose nearby nest it was. Much of what he requested is illegal nowadays, but I think his interests benefitted the avifauna overall. He and his knowledge fought unwelcome and anti-bird proposals (with his very personal form of tooth and claw) that might have made life difficult for some species in

130

particular. Would that he had seen frigates, and then been overjoyed, but – alas – he did not leave the British mainland. At least that meant I never had to climb within some frigate colony, having magnificence and tropical treetops all about me, while I gazed at each single nest containing its single pure white egg. (I had always thought that pure white eggs were only laid when a nest was in a hole, but the frigates break this rule, just as they do about almost everything.)

My father's zest for birds had been pre-empted in his life by an equally determined approach to moths. He preferred these to the gaudier butterflies, and would announce to inquisitive grown-ups that 'mothing' was his favoured business. Everything mothy was good for him and he was, in short, a mother. Most books deal with the lepidoptera in general; hence the great excitement when he found one day, and spontaneously bought at great pocket-money cost, *British Mothers*. He admitted later that the tome took time to get going, with health and exercise important adjuncts, but he ploughed on mainly because its single-minded Britishness made it doubly welcome as he had no wish for foreign moths when pursuing the sport of mothing. Alas, alas, as discerning readers may already have realized, he was suddenly confronted by baby talk, with extraordinary chapters concerning presentation, delivery, lactation and micturition – whatever these might be. Perhaps this was why he switched to birds, became a birder, bought birdy books and revelled in their bird-rich excellence for the remainder of his days.

With so much time available on the raft, and with so much solitude, I spent hours debating internally my father's style of life and mine. From the start of adulthood I had been driven by a built-in longing to see other places, to revel in them and experience the intensities they provided. My progenitor knew that Britain, or rather the various homes within southern England that came his way, gave him everything he needed.

131

There was affinity between him and, say, swallows. They did experience other places, if coming perhaps from Natal, but always returned to the same old eave on the same old barn. Why go anywhere else? Is anything better – for swallows or humans – than an English summer's evening when the feel of the air is just right, the thrush is belting out its song, the flowers that do so have shut up shop and there is perfection everywhere.

My father was one of nine children, two boys and seven girls, and they all felt equally – or so it seemed – that Britain was the place to be. They were generally born within its borders and, apart for some rare ventures elsewhere, they lived and died within them. Travel, of course, is easier nowadays but it was always possible for those with the necessary impetus. It so happened that my father's only brother was born in Baden Baden, and did spend a dozen later years in Iraq, but his final job and lengthy retirement were experienced back home. And so, I realized ruefully, would probably be my final days. Nevertheless I have tasted the waters elsewhere, again and again and again, with these forays always so very good.

I do not think my father ever began to understand foreign situations and foreign climates or indeed foreign anything. If I sent a letter his way from some arid area, it perhaps bemoaning a lack of rain for some two years, he would jauntily reply: 'Same here; the sprouts in particular need a good drenching.' If, contrarily, I was experiencing an hourly inch of rain for days on end he would tell 'of last Saturday's cricket being completely washed out'. I loved all these replies and I loved him. He was steadfast in his loyalties, and not bouncing from one desire to another as was generally my way. On the raft, pinioned from hopping elsewhere and forced within myself by the proximity of companions, I was happy to spend time with him as company, so to speak, and as I remembered him.

My mother, alas, was less appealing. It was 'typical of you to arrive when there was no one around to help', she chided

Anthony with flying fish

(Ali Porteous)

Andy learning to play the guitar

(Dave Hildred)

Antiki approaching St Maarten

Antiki crew after arrival on St Maarten

Antiki's hull had to be cleaned of barnacles in St. Maarten

Bruno adjusting the sail rigging

Nigel worries Bruno may fall in

(Bruno Sellmer)

Nigel, Ali, Leigh and Anthony relax in the cabin

(Bruno Sellmer)

Ali enjoying lunch

Anthony and Bruno sunbathing

Ali and Bruno row the dinghy out to take pictures

Ali lets off a flare as the storm blows *Antiki* towards the reefs

Anthony and Tony Humphries discussing stepping the mast

(Robin Batchelor)

Antiki is washed ashore on Eleuthera

Anthony about to set foot on Eleuthera after a very dramatic stormy arrival

when remembering the day of my emergence. I went on being 'typical' in her eyes, this word covering a feast of happenings but never flattering. She had been engaged at nineteen, married at twenty and gave birth to her first child within a year. Two more of us then arrived, keeping her occupied despite the presence of two staff. When we children had all departed for boarding school, the last when she was thirty-five, she seemed to realize that life, and being young, had somehow passed her by. What had happened to parties, to the 'season' and having fun? Her duty had been obeyed and her duty had let her down. She had twice gone abroad (with her mother) when still single, but her husband was never so inclined. There were always some purchased Renaissance prints about our house, such as a side-view portrait by Pollaiuolo, and she gave me Benvenuto Cellini's autobiography when I was young, each suggesting where her feelings lay vis-à-vis foreign travel, but there was no possibility of going abroad herself with such a husband as my father.

'When did my mother grow bitter?' I belatedly asked a great friend of hers one day.

Instead of dismissing such a question, it being both distasteful and unwelcome, that woman considered, without much pause for thought, the particular year of 1937 to have been most relevant. My mother did her duty all her life, and then fell over when widowed and aged eighty-eight, breaking her hip in the process.

'Now I want to die,' she said, and so she did just six days later.

With her ending, and her husband's earlier conclusion, a style of life had been terminated. She always spoke of 'saving the pennies' and I never learned of their actual financial situation. I only knew that, whatever the sums involved, these two parents would always economize. No light bulb ever shone in rooms they were not using or in the passageways. No food ever 'went to waste'; that was not a proper happening. Mattresses were turned over doggedly; that was how they should be treated. The house temperature was always low, whatever visitors might wish. The two of them dressed near the airing cupboard with its door ajar. That way they could enjoy a little extra heat and yet not squander it. They did not visit the local surgery 'because it was surely busy'. They were ideal as members of their community, never being demanding, never taking one mite more than was their due. Their style of economy used to be more general but was ridiculed by the young of subsequent generations. Nurtured in Victorian values, and aided by wartime shortages, their style is gone. Who now keeps boxes of saved items, such as rubber bands, short bits of string, a joint whose meat has been consumed, and thrice-mended socks or shirts whose amendments will 'make them last'. (I heard of one woman, plainly a sticker for throwing nothing good away, who left at her death a box labelled 'Pieces of String Not Worth Saving'. My mama and – to some extent papa – would have understood precisely.)

Of course I thought of these two parents and their kind of life on ordinary days back home, but I communed with them most lengthily and determinedly when travelling on the raft. There were the other three companions so close at hand but that very closeness had distanced me from them – if that makes sense. Whether it does or not I was glad to think deeply about those two predecessors of mine and found the act rewarding. In the solitude of a night's watch I did speak with them, apologized, expressed gratitude, remembered happy times, felt grateful for their creation of the person who was me and considered myself at one with them. Had they also spoken at these times I would have been excited, but not totally amazed. There was a proximity to them onboard the raft that was never known even when they were still alive. Very sad, but true.

12

The logbook that resided on the electronics desk was mainly compiled by David. He made most of the decisions and therefore had most to record. Every now and then he also summed up the existing situation, such as:

1,901 nm from La Gomera/Valle Gran Rey
1,556 nm to Bahamas
623 nm to Sint Maarten

Despite our resolution to head for proximity and nearby land, whether the wind 'strengthened' or 'lessened' during the subsequent days there were still surprises, such as 'Tracking west with a little south, but actually going east in a countercurrent.' I certainly found it disarming to be definitely sailing west – as indeed we were – but for our GPS to show movement in an easterly direction.

As for the island of Sint Maarten, its more desirable southern portion lay almost exactly on the eighteenth parallel. Therefore, should we be north or south of that latitude, we took prompt steps to realign ourselves more correctly. This meant adjustment to the yardarm, the sail, the guaras and the steering oar. By no means were we without control; instead we had a feast of it. It was impossible to know which mechanism

135

was being most effective, as with a doctor using drugs and surgery and optimistic talk, but we saw more point in a general use of course adjusters than choosing just the one.

At this stage in the journey the four guaras – our Peruvian steering aids – were becoming better understood, with the front pair thought to be less influential than those two at the rear. Each of the four were some two feet broad and six feet tall, with about four feet protruding beneath our bottom pipes when we were making use of them. The ancient guara users, so we had read, had some twenty or so upon each raft, these being their only means of steering. With them they would travel, for example, from the South American mainland even to Easter Island, a place 1,500 miles from anywhere else.

Not only did our four guaras assist with directional ability but, like keels, they hindered sideways drift. We thought it should be possible to navigate solely with such off-centre dagger boards, but did not do so. (How long was it after steam arrived before sails on ships were quite withdrawn?) As it was, and with us, we adjusted, tweaked, raised, lowered, tightened and slackened everything we had – including guaras – and then watched the GPS. It was belt, braces and also string. This did seem preferable. Someday a modern rafter will have to try them exclusively, as we were failing to do. I feel sure that success will partner such an act, however much we did not try the scheme ourselves.

When we set course for Sint Maarten, and therefore favoured 18 North, we were at 50 West or so. Therefore we had to travel through twelve more degrees of longitude before reaching our destination. This meant, perhaps, some ten more days of voyaging, with two knots persisting as average speed, but another depression, more backward currents or any new surprises could easily disrupt the estimated arrival time. We therefore relaxed, went about our chores, were totally confident in our raft, wondered how we had been quite so brilliant in putting the thing together, knew we had ample food, water and cooking gas onboard, and therefore deserved to be rapped on the knuckles for such overbearing confidence. Might not a whale rise up beneath us? Would illness strike? Would anything happen to shift our complete complacency?

It did not seem so. As it happened, the first change to come our way as we gradually neared the land was a single-engined aircraft. We could not speak with those onboard – the aviation and maritime worlds seem to operate different systems – but we assumed they were friends come to observe and perhaps take photographs. Anyhow they swooped and dived, flew alongside and directly overhead, and most raucously informed us that our transatlantic days were coming to an end. Going and gone were the tranquillity we had known so long. Instead the twenty-first century was noisily coming to meet us. We did not leap up and down with joy, as might have been expected. We merely sat and watched until the noisy intruder chose to fly away.

As for our course at that time David worried most, but only about our precise positioning. Any deviation from 18 North was pounced upon and put immediately correct. His reputation as a rafting sailing master would stand or fall in the next few hours. It had been presumptuous to be so precise with our given waypoint, but also correct to give it. After so many weeks of travelling, with the horizon uninterrupted by any form of land, it did seem a touch improbable that something solid might suddenly arise. The instruments said so, along with the saner portions of one's brain, but I could not imagine what such an alteration might look like and was almost frightened by the thought. 'Land Ho!' is the customary shout, and we shouted almost silently when an island came in view shortly after the sun had set on the second Tuesday following our forecast ten days earlier.

The lump of rock was huge. Why did we not see it earlier? It was not a very distant smudge but a hugely tall piece of upright land. There were lights on it, some of these moving, some flickering, and all emphasizing that the place was occupied. I stared and stared but Dave was more down to earth and certainly laconic.

'That's St Barts,' he said. 'Know it well.'

This was the first bit of land to be seen since La Gomera had vanished in our wake nine weeks earlier – or thereabouts as, during that early portion of our trip, we had looked forwards rather than behind and did not notice when the most westerly Canaries had finally disappeared. For all the days afterwards there had been only ocean on every side, and suddenly there was this formidable interruption. What was holding it there? More to the point, would we run into it, this single obstacle that had come our way?

'Fat chance,' said David. 'It's miles away.'

Having arrived, it then stayed virtually motionless. At last we had something by which to measure our modest haste. Two knots is less than walking speed, and mountains are slow in their arrival if you are only dawdling to reach them. We still seemed to be rushing, with the Atlantic rollers lifting our stern, passing noisily underneath and then hurrying forwards from our craft, but the instruments stuck to the facts. If St Barts was, say, fifteen miles away, and we were keeping to the same old speed, it would take us over seven hours, and almost the remainder of the night, before we reached that land. As it was we wished to journey past it and reach Sint Maarten, the island of our choice.

This other piece of land also arrived surreptitiously. One moment there was no such place. Then, mere seconds later, a new outline appeared on the horizon. Quite differently shaped to St Barts, the island of Sint Maarten was longer, wider and richer with illumination. It was also quite far away. So we

138

carried on, with thoughts greatly mixed about the ending of our trip, and listened to the waves urging us towards the spot that we had chosen, that waypoint proudly given some ten days earlier. The darkness grew more absolute as the night deepened, and the four of us onboard stared blankly at the nothingness all about us. Like being in an aircraft at 30,000 feet and then looking down, there was only our immediate surroundings and then nothing else but water, save for that backdrop of an isle. It was all so unreal and yet we were charging onwards with extraordinary intent.

David still continued to fuss about our actual direction, moving the lengthy rudder just a little touch from time to time. We could see each other well enough, with all the cabin lights switched on, but the surrounding darkness gave little clue about the community straight ahead. A few bright flashes indicated no-go areas, perhaps because of reefs or other hazard. We could not hope to steer between them – the necessary changes in direction being too sensitive an operation for a raft – but they were still quite a way in front of us. So would there be assistance waiting at our waypoint, this given to the island ten days earlier? The nearer we drew to Sint Maarten the greater grew our concerns. It was all very well just driving ahead, with the waves keeping up their urgent power, but there would have to be help before too long. In fact, it would be crucial within a hundred yards or so as the gap diminished between us and 18.12 North plus 63.21 West. Very quickly, or so we thought, and right now would do.

'Hello *Antiki*. We are Search and Rescue,' was then loud-hailered to us with a soft Dutch accent from the darkness all around.

That I suddenly did not want. Such formal assistance often comes at a price, as I knew from previous experiences. Help does not always come for free.

'Hello to you. We have no need of Search and Rescue and are in good order.'

'Hello *Antiki*,' came the immediate reply. 'We are Search and Rescue with cold beer.'

With that we suddenly saw boats on either side of us, these packed with people all yelling and shouting in our direction. The search and rescuers were soon alongside, proffering the promised drink, and our fingers were quickly grasping this welcome offering. We also lowered our sail, there being no need for further shove from wind. The end had therefore arrived so very speedily. From charging along in standard fashion, urged forward by breeze and current, we were putting ourselves in other hands. The four of us had been in control for sixty-five days, ever since the tow rope had been discarded so very bluntly just beyond the harbour of Valle Gran Rey. Now, and with the lowered sail, we were relinquishing that authority. It was like being lifted from an accident, tended by helpful hands and rested on a stretcher. The problem – our problem – had been donated elsewhere. We merely had to sip the beer.

The whoops continued from the accompanying craft, informing us who was shouting and telling us of their joy. David's wife Trish was there, having flown from nearby Tortola. Andy's wife Beryl was also there, having travelled from faraway Alberta, Canada. All sorts of other people, from the yacht club and from the government, were onboard shouting out their names. And photographers were certainly there, blinding us again and again with their bright and flashing cameras. It was all so very joyous, so welcoming, such fun. On the other hand, I was not truly welcoming all that merriment.

Those onboard the rescue boat were doing what was necessary, positioning themselves at our prow, gathering our rope, fixing it most properly and then taking up the slack. Soon we were experiencing quite a different form of motion, being independent of the waves. Simpson's Bay was quickly straight ahead, the place we had seen from books and charts as a desirable spot for anchorage. It was certainly not rafting territory as we were made to snake our way past other craft pinioned to their buoys. Ahead we saw the lights and bustle of a town while, as if magically, we were manoeuvred past millions of dollars' worth of yacht. An empty buoy, plainly prearranged, was then ahead and soon we were as captive as all the other craft. The enormous journey from one side of the Atlantic to the other had thereby been concluded. *Antiki* was at rest.

It was now midnight, more or less. David and Andy disembarked to meet their waiting wives, and all the other boats vanished with them. John and I were therefore on our own, not so much keeping guard as seeing no point in going ashore. It is hard to imagine now, or even remember, the glee for the two of us at finding ourselves alone. At last, at long last, we could talk about the others and about the trip with a freedom quite impossible during the previous nine weeks. We were not malicious in our chat; we were merely revealing personal thoughts without fear of offending some nearby pair of ears. 'Do you remember when . . .' vied with 'Wasn't it odd that . . .' and these reflections kept us going deep into that night. I suppose some of the speech was snide but so much thought had been cooped up for some 2,400 miles. At all events we talked and talked, and the night went on and on.

Almost at once I resented our actual situation in that bay. We had struggled so hard to get there and I, for one, did not like the world that we had finally reached. There was unpleasant music coming from some darkened café, the noise made worse by the distortions of loud-speakering. There were bright lights of advertisements telling that I should buy fruit, drink, change my home, acquire a car and insure the family. One cannot be against such recommendations but, inanely and to no one in particular at that hour, they jabbered their flickering

141

messages without cease. Similarly there were cars travelling in each direction. Why so much coming and going? Why not just stay put?

I suppose this was all response to the wonder of being at sea. The ocean had been a place of innocence, with a purity that did not exist on land – or rather on a land so beset with human interference. We four had all been privileged; no doubt about that. We had lived with and on another kind of world. It had supported us and charmed us. It had shown us sights we had never seen before, and had caused us to have thoughts that were quite new in our experience. Meeting land again was like encountering some drunk when strolling arm in arm with one's beloved. Having it all around, as within that bay, was not appealing. It was the kind of world in which I customarily lived, but the raft had taken me elsewhere, had given different insights, and had been a great intensity. The dark, cold, empty desolation had been astonishing. Eliot had been quite right, and we had been quite right in travelling by raft for all that length of time. The sadness, as I then thought, lay in the termination. At all events, with the flickering neon still undiminished, the café still wretchedly raucous, and our two heads most confused by the novel happenings, we called it a day at 3.30 and turned in, as the saying goes, to get some sleep.

Other individuals had different ideas about when the new day should dawn. At six o'clock there came a shout – did we want some bread? A few minutes later there came another – did we wish for local newspapers? What we did desire was coffee, and this we drank from our stock until we learned what had been planned for us. Apparently, in order to enter the lagoon and reside within its security, a road bridge had to be raised so that masted vessels could enter safely. We were in that category and would be towed inwards at the 5.30 p.m. opening, these things scheduled in advance. Andy and David then came back, talking merrily of hotel breakfasts and we all prepared *Antiki* for her more public arrival. A space had apparently been reserved for us at the yacht club's own marina, and there we would stay for the initial week, on show as it were for all to see.

When afternoon arrived there came a towing boat. Dave took up position by the steering oar, Andy readied his camera, John climbed on the cabin's roof, as he plainly wished to do and I prepared to film. All was therefore set for our formal arrival, as against being merely positioned on a little buoy. Soon we could see that the road ahead was being lifted vertically, and our towing craft prepared itself – and us – to pass beneath. Andy was clicking away, and I too tried to film this novel entranceway. Suddenly there were great hoots from, presumably, the colossal yachts moored nearby and also great shouts from people. What was happening? Who – and where – were all these individuals? With one eye on the camera my other saw a great crowd, yelling its head off, whistling, cheering, waving and competing in its decibels with those foghorn hoots so blasted in our direction. The Sint Maarten Yacht Club, no less, was heralding our arrival in no uncertain manner. It was shouting fit to bust.

It took a little time to be manoeuvred to that honoured place reserved for our arrival. A young boy, barefooted in true Tom Sawyer style, first stared and then surfaced with a question.

'Good 'eavens, how old are you?'

On being answered he shouted that his 'gramp' of equal age 'never even bothered to go out'. Other people shouted greetings, along with questions asking how and when and why and who and where. We tied up, with people on every side. There were hugs – oh yes, there were hugs – and all my dismal feelings about meeting land again were being vanished with each one, whether from male, female, big, small, huge or most desirable. People were what I had missed, people in all their variety, lovely, lovely people in whatever shape or form. Gradually we four were edged on shore, or rather by that floating dock, and then were bustled up a ramp to meet the place where drinks were merrily available. More hugs now that we were sitting down, more enthusiasm and more joy. We had been asked earlier of our wishes for land-based meal No.1, and three steaks were soon in front of us to partner the omelette that I preferred. Talk, greetings, wishes, laughter – it all went on and on deep into that amazing evening.

Eventually there came the matter of accommodation. David and Andy departed with their ladies while John and I, hardly bereft of company, were invited by a man named Alan Bishop to rest up at his home.

'It's on the French side,' he explained as we relaxed within his car, not that we cared or even wondered where he might be driving us.

The evening was just being great, whatever happened or would happen as we were being transported to his home. This proved to be a most substantial dwelling, full of space and tall ceilings – and so wildly different from a corrugated cabin that had served us for so long. In my room, with its glass doorways, lightweight curtaining, a colossal bed and the smoothest of floors, I wondered why – and with such effort – I had thought a raft desirable even for a single evening, let alone such a quantity of days. I looked into the shower room, knew for sure it would work perfectly and deliver neither hot nor cold excessively as showers so often do. Excellence was all about me and I wasted no time in taking off what few clothes I wore. These were dismissed with happy disregard as I walked towards the shower. My body had not seen its like for weeks and weeks, and I stepped into its considerable waterfall knowing that life was being perfect, with the temperature being perfect, the warm torrent quite correct and wonder everywhere.

Only then, when sudden silence reigned, did I remember about my hearing aid. How pathetic and idiotic! How dotty! And how very, very stupid! I had looked after the thing most earnestly during every day afloat. And now I had just destroyed it as it had gone quiet instantaneously.

'We'll just play everything by hearing aid,' I had jested when problems were in view and now, through total happiness, I had killed the thing stone dead.

Electricity and water do not mix, however modest the power consumed, however small the thing involved. And all because I had been in post-raft ecstasy – the room, the bed, the floor and all those hugs so recently received. Oh well, as *Gone with the Wind* concluded so famously, tomorrow is another day.

13

Amazingly, in that such things should not happen, the aid worked perfectly on the following morning. Something like a hairdryer is normally necessary – and speedily – to remove all water, but the dry warmth of Sint Maarten had done the trick quite perfectly. However there were many more tricks the island had to do. What could be arranged for the raft once that week of demonstration had been concluded? We had made great play of the fact that 2,478 miles had been accomplished in sixty-six extraordinary days, but one more mile or so was necessary to meet a berth where our great raft could be deployed. Everyone was being helpful, certainly Alan Bishop as host and an amazing woman named Petra, tireless manager of the Sint Maarten Yacht Club.

Almost at once we were informed of a man named Guy. He owned a barren piece of land that was powerfully patrolled, and most comprehensively, by his pack of dogs. These five were, allegedly, far more effective in guarding property than any security system, however costly, however top of the range. The empty area of their territory was entirely to our liking. The raft could be pulled from the water, manoeuvred over a little bank of sand, and then dragged to some dead ground perfectly suited for our vessel. We only needed to hire a digger to pull us to shore, acquire some pipes to ease the travelling, and then store *Antiki* for as long as necessary. Dog food was not even to be paid. Guy kept his animals well supplied with that, causing them to sit and scratch contentedly while the raft safety they ensured was properly discussed. As recompense for all this hospitality, we gave Guy and his canine pack several boxes of unused Tesco food from England, our 'victual' supplier having done her job too well.

'The church will be very grateful,' he said, and took merry charge of our offerings.

So how long would the raft have to stay under the ten watchful eyes of canine security? I still hankered for Eleuthera, the Bahamian island where those two British sailors had landed in 1940. Their astonishing voyage had lasted for seventy days and had been powerful inspiration, just seventy-one years later, for my own enterprise. That ambition had then proved to be impossible, with work requirements for the crew getting in the way, and indeed my own medication needs of daily pills because my onboard supply was ending, but the intended destination still existed at the back of my mind. It then was pushed to the front, most firmly, when broadcasting channels and a publishing house stated independently that my project was only half achieved if I got no further than Sint Maarten. There were still, they insisted, another 800 miles and perhaps another month of travelling before the job could be considered done. Money would not be available from their coffers unless the venture ended properly. Everest, in short, still had to be climbed in full.

After a few days of rejoicing, and welcoming the island's hospitality, the other three then chose to go back home. They did not possess my pig-headed desire and, once the Atlantic had been crossed, believed the journey to be completed. I reminded them of the solemn declaration we had all made, before crowning it with Dorado beer, and that Eleuthera was our goal, but they considered that matter terminated now that we had, as it were, hit town. What with Dave and John having work to do, with good homes and former lives to go to, they all wanted the old days once again, much as they had been before even hearing of Valle Gran Rey. Consequently David soon returned to the Virgin Islands, Andy to Canada and John to his home near Oxford plus his desk at nearby Stroud. My raft crew had been assembled, not without difficulty. This rafting crew had then vanished homewards with no problem whatsoever. Therefore yet another *Mary Celeste* had once more been created.

It was all very well for possible paymasters to insist upon the journey's second leg but that achievement would be far less straightforward. As David had insisted, along with his steady reminders of the greater distance to be achieved, the business of heading north-west rather than due west would be a great deal trickier. The east/west trade winds blowing from Africa to the Indies become confused when meeting land, whether it was islands big or small. In any case the Gulf of Mexico has no exit and the transatlantic simplicity becomes a deal more complex. For one thing – and a very big thing it was – the standard wind assaulting travellers heading north-west from the Leewards tended to blow unhelpfully from the north-east. It was possible, as we had learned, for *Antiki* to receive and act upon breezes arriving on her beam, and be made to navigate without drifting inexorably sideways, but that does not mean we had no wish for a wind to blow more directly at our stern.

The Bahamas could have more easily been reached from that decision point 600 miles east of land where we had chosen to forget Eleuthera. We could have crabbed from there in a west-north-west fashion more readily than hoping to steer north-west when wind direction was even less appealing. Therefore the plan, when heading from Sint Maarten, would be to go north as much as possible before turning west, having reached Eleuthera's latitude. Time would tell whether this wish was feasible or merely impossible. It did look, with bits and pieces of islands along the route, as if the task of travelling by raft from our halfway stopping place to my desired destination was out of the question. David had done well in crossing the Atlantic. Whoever took on the second journey would have to do better still. Somehow I would have to find such an individual and that would take some time.

At all events, having so recently arrived at our chosen place, it being an interval, I took increasing advantage of the island's merits. The French half does actually speak French and does have better food. The Dutch portion is somewhat cheaper and English is the language used. With new friends I ate, of course, at the Kon-Tiki restaurant. We picnicked in places that my children, in long gone days, would have treasured absolutely, so rich were they with pools and sand and gentle bursts of waves. There were parties to enjoy in houses, not so much near a beach as directly on one. I acquired more pills from a most amiable doctor, his surgery possessing four upright tubes much like frankfurters, these indicating different rigidities for the human penis – making a remarkable sight and astonishing feel I had never seen or felt before. The island of St M. (as some call it) manufactures nothing, or so it seems, and grows nothing, but certainly milks all visitors of cash. These people arrive, perhaps, as modest sailors, or upon gigantic yachts without a sail in sight, or – far more importantly – from cruise liners which, with decks beyond number well above the water-line, are able to release some 6,000 passengers happy to lighten their wallets however they may choose. St M. is a very happy place; at least I found it so. The queue of cars ahead may be long and slow-moving, but the sun is shining, the sky is blue, the vistas are spectacular and palm trees do have a peculiar excellence. And is that not the bar or restaurant straight ahead that we are heading for?

THIRTEEN

No one at the yacht club, however affable, offered themselves as potential crew, let alone as sailing master, for the
second voyage. I even pinned up notices but nobody accepted.
Ah well, the choice would have to wait. By arriving in April
there was not much time before dreadful hurricanes might
wage war against all humans and their property, particularly if
this was some kind of boat still afloat just waiting to be blown
to bits. June is the earliest month for these strong 'blows' to
do their thing, and sea water has to reach twenty-eight degrees
Celsius before they can begin. Travelling from St M. northwards would be sufficiently perplexing without having to listen
on the radio for news of terrifying hurricanes. On the other
hand, this frightening form of season, lasting at least until
September's end, gave me good reason for delay. When
enjoying Sint Maarten, and after delicately admiring those
frankfurter firmnesses and the cafes and the restaurants and
all the parties, I had some five months of time during which
to gather a different crew. The raft was not yet under dog control but everything had been prepared, the money donated,
the digger identified and old poles discovered to ease our
raft's happy progress over land. Locks had also been acquired
to keep the cabin's contents safe, and there was nothing more
for me to do. Therefore I purchased an air ticket, discovered
that London via Miami and Boston formed the cheapest route,
and settled down to be cramped and miserable for all the
hours before Heathrow came my way.

14

It was good to have returned. Friends and family existed, and their different company was great. I tried to tell these others of the intensities that had occurred, of frigate birds and shear-waters, of the ocean itself and what it had given me. I much enjoyed the day of speaking at WaterAid's annual jamboree. A large audience, learning terrible information about unneces-sary death, was made eager to work yet harder following great speeches that promoted such a vital cause. When I spoke they relished the opportunity to laugh for a change, particularly at some of the rafting antics which had come our way. I was subsequently applauded and back-thumped for the achieve-ment of crossing the Atlantic, and tried to explain that sitting on a chair to watch a watery world go by was hardly laudable when compared with digging wells for the most precious liquid of them all. People channelling clean water, cutting down dis-ease, improving sanitation and spending money wisely were those among the audience needing praise, but I did not object when applause came my way as I told of other things. After all those frightening revelations of infant mortality, plus pictures of young ribs seen so very visibly, the delegates would have laughed had I read from railway timetables as a form of light relief. As it was I felt delighted that WaterAid had been our chosen charity. The Aiders do such fine work, and are so humble about their labour, that it was an honour to be linked with them and to have put some cash their way.

'So what's happening next?' asked a couple of the thumpers. 'Will you continue to the Bahamas as you first desired or call it a day and rest?'

Television and the book business repeated that I had not achieved my goal. They said I had only reached Camp 6, or thereabouts, en route to Everest. In fact I was behaving as if such an intermediate achievement was quite sufficient when it was nothing of the sort. At least I should 'try' to finish the job, this being my mother's frequent admonition when things were difficult. Failure – to her – was in consequence worthier than abandonment. I explained to my detractors that a new crew would have to be recruited but they were adamant. I told of extra expenditure, the necessary re-victualling, a determined inspection of the raft (for locating breakage) and the hazard in travelling north-west from Sint Maarten to Eleuthera, this far more difficult than being puffed from behind across the broad Atlantic. I told at length, but should have saved my breath. I even explained that telling of the new individuals onboard would resemble some disarming novel, possibly from Russia, where all the earlier characters are replaced by quite another horde for no good reason. The threesome of David, Andy and John had gone, as was their desire, and another set would have to take their place. Did this make any sense?

Whether it did or not suddenly became sidelined. News arrived from Sint Maarten with the dreadful haste so very possible these days – *Antiki* was adrift. By then the raft had not been towed to be guarded by tooth and claw. It had not even been placed on dry land, as another possibility had surfaced from a neighbouring marina. In fact nothing had happened save for the raft escaping from its anchor. Strong wind had caused the break, and that same vicious blow was reportedly playing with our twelve tons of raft as if something fun to do.

There were countless costly yachts within that lagoon, some being the mega-yachts of great size and worth. They all had price tags to bankrupt the owner of any free-range projectile about to do its worst against any hull that came its way. Of course I sent off emails. They went to everyone I knew who might know of a boat with sufficient power to halt the runaway and that, on an island so dominated by water craft, meant virtually everyone.

'*Antiki* is adrift, please help,' was the gist of all my pleading. 'Something must be done.'

Of course the raft was not insured, against third party or anything similar. Premiums would have been impossibly high and I had not bothered to ask. The Spanish at the Canary Islands had insisted upon insurance but only against personal injury, personal sickness and the like. They had no wish to pick up bills should one of us fall ill. This requirement I had arranged for the transatlantic crossing, but all such cover had ceased when that voyage had been completed. Consequently, should the raft damagingly collide – with anything – while on the rampage, it was easy to know where the repair bills would arrive. I thought it frightening even to open up my mail. It might, if fortune favoured, tell that the raft had been controlled or, contrarily and far less happily, could be from some unknown addressee talking of collision. But I still tapped in 'Send' for further unhappy messages from one very worried owner of a raft flouting its new-found liberty so disarmingly.

'Please help. Please capture the raft somehow. I will pay the towing bill.'

I did not know how much money would be involved should contact occur with some gin-palace of a yacht but presumed that raft-towing would be less, and lower than astronomical. In London, and at my desk, I fretted abjectly as if this was the only thing to do and even thought personal sanity might be diminishing. The sun shone brightly above my home but I mimicked a pitch-black cloud when that raft – my raft – was on the loose. When would this nightmare cease?

It did then cease but gave me further worry. (Is there a mental malaise where worries increase much like secondaries merely because time has passed and neglect has been excessively prolonged?) In any case I did – belatedly – receive good news. Eventually I learned that a tug had rescued my wandering property before attaching it to an anchor point used for cruise ships. So how much does one tug cost, per hour, per minute? And what about anchorages which keep big ships safe? The only person not to tell me of tug rescue was the tugboat man himself. So would I first hear from him when invoices were being despatched? Presumably he also owned the fastening that held my craft in check, something he could not now use, it being occupied. Should I even thank him, or his organization, thereby bringing the matter forward in his mind? In short, there are problems with worry-mania. It does progress; it can enslave and it will multiply.

Time passed and no tug message came. I began to breathe more freely and reverted to another concern – from where and how would I find a crew? The same old excuses bubbled up again – 'seasick all the way', 'Jenny wouldn't like me to', 'my employers need me', 'I need them'. I then remembered Bruno Sellmer. He, some thirty years ago, had been with me when eight of us had sailed on a steam-powered craft which, at three magnificent knots – or six when travelling downstream – covered some 2,000 miles of the mighty Araguaia river before it met the yet mightier Amazon. I had seen him catching snakes merely, it seemed, by walking up them from their tail. He sometimes stayed with me in London, abjuring the bed made up for him and sleeping on the floor. Plainly a man with modest needs which, even though he was now fifty, might have stayed with him.

'Dear Bruno, Will you come onboard my raft?'

154

'Yes, and I'll bring my hammock,' he replied, thus making it seem that not everything had changed in the intervening span.

A godchild of mine named Nigel Gallaher, British born but also American by marriage, had very recently been made redundant – receiving two weeks' severance pay (ye gods, that much!) after twenty-five years of employment with the same architecture company. I thought he might welcome another kind of life, and knew he was a part-time sailor. 'Yes,' was his reply, with the offer of his wife Leigh as extra, she too a sailor if given opportunity. The gender barrier was therefore removed, and so helped to add Alison Porteous to the new raft-membership. She would serve as camera-person, the film exposed thus far having all been shot by me. It therefore, however good or bad, was short of material concerning the leader of the enterprise, and this needed to be rectified. Her career had been as war specialist, taking a movie camera wherever life was difficult, and certainly with the rebel groups hiding in Ugandan forest who hoped to topple Idi Amin. After that man had abdicated she purchased an island – as one does – of great size in Lake Victoria, and let its visitors give her loot. Her answer to my enquiry just said, 'Yes, please, Yes, please,' and I put a tick against her name. Five people instead of four – so what? Two of them being women – so what again? I now had a crew. It was therefore Goodbye to Dave, John and Andy. It was also Hello to Bruno, Nigel, Leigh and Ali, you are very welcome on the raft and have totally plugged the gap.

What my newcomers did not know, but would quickly learn, was that the second of *Antiki's* journeyings would be so much harder than the first. They were happy to follow the transatlantic team but did not immediately comprehend that, in forsaking Eleuthera and settling for Sint Maarten, the wish to reach the Bahamas had become far more difficult. Had we opted for Eleuthera when 600 miles east of the nearest land, and when that confrontation had ended with its three-to-one decision, the Bahamian island of my desire was then – more or less – west-north-west of us. Unfortunately, and from Sint Maarten (as already mentioned), the angle had become a great deal sharper, being approximately north-west. With the expected winds shifting from easterly to nearer north-easterly the business of navigation would be much more demanding. It might not even be possible, if winds were almost always on our beam, to reach that island of Eleuthera which had always been my dream. We might even travel west of it if we could not crab to the north sufficiently. Therefore we would not then make a landing, as the two sailors had achieved, on the island's eastern side. That, to my besotted mind, would be a major disappointment.

In the middle of March 2012 I saw no reason for staying in England any longer. Therefore, via Miami, I took flight for Sint Maarten. Petra, the yacht club's manager and previous fixer of so much, was there to meet me, making the venture doubly pleasing. Of course she questioned about the new crew, saddened that three old friends, Dave, John and Andy, were no longer to be seen. Instead, as I explained, Bruno from Sao Paulo would be first to come, Ali would then arrive from her Ugandan home, and Nigel plus Leigh would be last to arrive after coming south from (relatively) nearby Boston. The two of us then repaired, as the saying goes, to a Chinese food place run by an Englishman where we relished the sand between our toes. Sint Maarten, as ever, was an enchanting place to be.

There was certainly much to do. The raft, still on its big ship buoy, needed to be extracted from the water, cleaned of the ecological mayhem growing underneath, replaced at some nearby quayside and generally prepared for Voyage No.2. The Sint Maarten Boatyard, and its owner Mervyn, instantly offered everything – removal from water with a massive and mobile hunk of machinery, pipe cleaning with high-powered jet, and replacement at a dockside with water and electricity on tap nearby. Final towing out to sea would be no problem once the others had arrived. In many ways it was therefore Valle Gran Rey all over again, save that St M. was yet more generous, that hurricanes would loom if we delayed too long, that the yacht club was a splendid watering hole, and I wondered why I should ever leave. What was wrong with growing roots, having encountered such a lovely place?

Bruno then arrived, and with a feast of camera boxes as photography was his business and he wished to exploit his skills. It was dark when he surfaced at the airport, and first stop was the raft. It did look well in the moonlight and also in the playback system that cameras use these days. (What has happened to the ancient joy of emerging from a pharmacy, extracting the prints from their pocket opposite the negatives and yelling 'They've come out!' – if indeed they had?) We then repaired, yet again, to the sand plus Anglo-Chinese mix that had already served us well.

There is a law which states, however much ignorance exists on one's own side, that it is easy to see if others know what they are doing. Fakery or cover-up sticks out a mile, with pretence at ability totally conspicuous. Bruno touched everything on the raft as if he had created it. He fingered the sail, gripped the ropes, muttered to himself, questioned items, nodded at others, and was instantly at home in a place he had never seen before. Everything was photographed, admired or criticized, lifted or let be, and fully understood before that first day was done. He then found attachment points for his hammock, made the cotton thing look far more comfortable than any bunk, and was soon asleep.

Ali Porteous turned up some three days later. I had written down the hour of her arrival wrongly (by some six hours) and was therefore absent when she emerged from customs. This did not greatly trouble the oh-so-resourceful woman. Having realized my absence she found a taxi, gave an arm-waving

157

description of the raft in general to its unblinking driver and was soon by my elbow drawing attention to herself. Guilt bubbled within me – but not for long; she had arrived and that was all that mattered. Very quickly she too was busy with her movie camera and overjoyed at everything she saw, such as the raft, the surrounding hospitality, the merits of Sint Maarten and, of course, the management called Petra. It was not so much a joining of new crew as a dovetailing, a binding and a meshing that had been far less apparent with the previous assortment of different individuals. I was therefore mighty pleased.

Last to arrive was the duo who had travelled least. All of us (and Petra) went to meet them at the airport on the very first day of April 2012. Of course they had only purchased single tickets, not knowing from which other island they might eventually return. This had caused trouble, with their arrival resembling immigration, but time had been spent successfully in resolving that issue. We waiting foursome had almost given up hope of finding those we wished to meet when they surfaced wearily. Anyway, great! *Antiki*'s new team had finally been assembled.

'Are we leaving first thing tomorrow?' asked the two from Boston. 'We certainly hope so.'

I explained that many 'last minute' items needed to be acquired, such as the perishable food – potatoes, fruit, bread and the like. Leigh had already taken great care in suggesting menus with healthy nourishment. Therefore it seemed pre-arranged that she should help with the final foody purchases. This she did with energy, and soon numerous items were arriving at the raft which I had never contemplated. There were delicious honeydew melons and, beating them for size, several watermelons resembling footballs which they do. The many kinds of vegetable were all pleasingly chilled and there were numerous cartons of eggs.

'We two always have boiled eggs for breakfast,' said Leigh, 'and know it would be wrong to change.'

It did seem as if the Boston lifestyle was being replicated, in so far as this was possible. I therefore thought about 'adventure' and what this meant precisely. Leigh said it was a hallenge, and I asked what she might miss most on the raft. A dishwasher was her answer, giving me more cause for thought. On the other hand it could have been a joke mocking my questioning. In any case what is wrong with helpful items; why should they be denied? If crossing the Sahara, for example, why sleep on sharp-edged stones? If mattresses are available why not sleep on them, and listen as one lay there to the dishes being washed. The earlier rafting venture had been more spartan. This new one would be different, of that I was suddenly sure.

Last-minute activity went on and on. Bruno was introduced to some extraordinary software for helping him with navigation, it having by then been decided that he would be the sailing master. (This was never argued; it just seemed correct.) A company named Budget Marine gave us a reconditioned 40 hp outboard engine and we bought some fuel for it. This acquisition went against the grain with my desire to travel only by current and whatever wind existed, but there was no need to use the thing, it serving in its way as second parachute. Anyhow a transom was built for it and we were excited by the gift. David Hildred flew over from his Virgin home and was extremely useful trying to spot possible damage to the raft. Ali filmed all the happenings, and Nigel and Leigh were helpful wherever needed. Bruno leaped from photography to everything else, and I sat on my chair, that thing filched from our Canary apartment so very long ago. There was no need for baptism on this second voyage and, almost abruptly, no need to wait any more. A towing boat arrived and it pulled us from the quay. Those on the colossal catamaran expensively parked next door on the quay were presumably still asleep, but they had not been greatly interested either in us or our craft. In any case we were soon back on the Atlantic where we more properly belonged.

There were immediate major differences, apart from the brand-new crew. The cabin was a lot tidier and the food a great deal tastier. Rightly or wrongly the old edict that everyone on deck should wear harness, and this should be clipped to the circular fastening to prevent seaward tumbling, became disregarded. Neither Bruno nor Ali, such independent spirits, could see the point and I acquiesced. In any case Bruno relished being elsewhere, swimming at the very end of that twenty-five-foot oar – to change its fastening, sitting astride a nose cone to attach one sail-rope as far forwards as possible and just being in the water. Leigh and Nigel, having gone to work on their eggs, were diligent with assistance wherever necessary. All, in fact, looked good.

One huge dissimilarity to the earlier trip was that we were soon travelling on the western side of an island lying almost in our path. Known as Sombrero, we never even saw it, as we passed at night, but it was there all right, lying to the east of us. Had it been possible we would have preferred all land to be to the westward, and for us to travel at a much more northerly angle, but that was not just difficult – it was quite beyond our powers. With a wind blowing from the north-east it was all we could do to have much northing in our course, with north-west the best that we could manage – or rather as three of us could. I made notes and watched but poor Nigel learned quickly where and how to vomit, his *mal de mer* so promptly dominant. He took pills, of course, and used – I think – a patch, but he was considerate in his jettisonings and laboured diligently whenever and however this was feasible.

His wife thought and demanded that he should eat, and eat he did, but the gain soon became loss when he went back to the side again.

Someone said, most unkindly, that he was helping nearby fishes but it could also be argued that his donations were keeping them all away. Not a single dorado came to keep us company, as had happened with such joy for the previous four of us. Our plankton hauls were also desultory when compared with the previous acquisitions. No barnacles grew on our nose cones, as they had done so profusely on Voyage No.1, perhaps encouraging energetic pilot fish, small and striped, to dart unceasingly among them. These creatures were swift to colonize on the previous trip, but no pilot fish darted about now. No sea birds came to visit us, not even the shearwaters and frigates that had been so plentiful and such joy. In other words that bit of sea was a desert by comparison, being also quite without dolphins or any of their tribe. Some ocean areas are so replete with food that fishermen flock, and always have flocked, to those regions. It seemed, contrarily, as if a kind of nothingness existed in this new area on which we five then sailed. There is talk of upwelling currents bringing nourishment from below, and far less of down currents doing no such thing. At least that was how it seemed to one group of rafters puzzled by the emptiness. There was even far less phosphorescence of the kind I had before enjoyed.

With two Americans onboard our raft, the subjects being discussed, either at meal times or when talk became appropriate, often concerned the USA. Outsiders can be amazed at that nation's love of personal guns and the huge number of accidental gun deaths that result. Similarly the fondness for driving almost everywhere, either to a neighbour's home or to the next-door parking lot, can worry non-Americans but not, or so it would seem, those car drivers who consume 40 per cent of the world's gasoline and kill some 50,000 fellow citizens when doing so. I – in particular – also mentioned the Pilgrim Fathers, wondering why they were so revered, when (as author Bill Bryson has phrased it) they 'packed as if misunderstanding the purpose of their trip' by finding room for sundials, candle-snuffers, a drum, a trumpet and a complete history of Turkey but none for a cow, a horse, a plough, a fishing line. They, as B. B. added, 'demonstrated their manifest incompetence in the most dramatic possible way – by dying in droves'. In April 1621, when the *Mayflower* returned to England, half of its former passengers were dead. Two English-speaking Indians – of all amazements – came to give the survivors help and, from that moment, only one other person died. I spoke merrily on this theme, having once researched it, but it was suddenly made plain that I had gone too far. Leigh lent across the table, rested on her hands, had anger in her eyes and lots of words to say.

'Why are you always attacking America? Is it because you lost your colonies and are jealous because you're no longer top dog?'

With that she hurried from the cabin, leaving great silence where she had been. I did then realize, plainly belatedly, that – with earlier mention of many US states favouring the death penalty, with Texas being particularly active in this regard, and concern that fifty million Americans have no health insurance – I had gone too far. Such criticism would not do within the confines of a raft. It would not do anywhere if susceptibilities, by being blatantly ignored, were severely injured. I therefore welcomed her back, grovelled as best I could and apologized most deeply. As captains go I had not gone properly, and life with Leigh was – alas – never quite the same again.

This was a shame. Nigel, still vomiting, was in the middle. Bruno and Ali helped to keep the peace, with Bruno a perfect diplomat. An underlying problem, not appreciated until both Bostonians were onboard, lay in their consumerism – and here

I go again. We had much water in the crosswise pipes, but were surprised at the rate they used it. We had paper tissues in abundance but they were used determinedly, being lifted from boxes in multiples rather than singletons. Above all they used electricity, with their particular diseases lying at the root. They both had 'problems' that made life difficult.

Leigh had bronchiectasis and had suffered from it for fifteen years. This made her cough – frequently. On land it forbade visits to the theatre, the cinema or concerts because her very audible coughing could become uncontrollable. On a raft it was merely annoying, to everyone as well as Leigh. One longed for her to cough up whatever formed the irritant but her inability to do so was the underlying difficulty. Whether pulmonary cilia were failing or her bronchi were too wide, she 'couldn't get the gunk up', as medical chums later explained to me. She had to use a nebulizer which passed air through albuterol at certain daytime hours. During these occasions she did crossword puzzles from a book and, oddly to my mind, looked up answers at the back when stuck for a certain word. She also experienced 'pummelling' from Nigel to serve as respiratory therapy, this sounding loud and painful. I do know this is a book about Atlantic rafting and not a medical treatise but Leigh's problem affected all of us. It also consumed considerable energy from our twelve-volt batteries. She felt, when questioned, that, 'one must never pass up an opportunity for adventure'. I felt a parallel pang at this desire for new experience and therefore warmed to her. The bronchial problem must be far more worrying, annoying and discouraging than my surgical metal hip.

Nigel's difficulty, apart from casting bread, and much else, upon the waters, was sleep apnoea. This sounds frightening, as it means the cessation of breathing during sleep. A sufferer can therefore hope the body is itself sufficiently disturbed by such awesome lack to wake up, and somehow kickstart the system into action once again, but there is also a machine, a 'continuous positive applied pressure device' (or CPAP) which can help. Its use, as we all noticed, meant retiring to sleep with a plastic face-mask plus suitable gadgetry and a fan to keep the temperature acceptable. This all led to yet more electrical demand. On a normal day, and when the sun had shone brightly on our four solar panels, the two batteries were left rich with energy. If the day had been overcast, and the batteries had been under-supplied, a great noise was subsequently emitted, this being a sort of death rattle from those batteries and an urgent cry for help. The wind generator was then switched on, our belt that went with braces, and – provided there was wind – it saved the situation. America could then have all the power it needed.

The arrival, and the use, of considerable medical equipment so near at hand (and ear and eye) caused thoughts to emerge and chat to surface about medical care in the US. Nigel told that over $2,000 a month kept his health insurance operational. Consequently, should a medical adviser recommend costly machinery which 'might be beneficial', it was easy for the insurance payer to accept such advice because blood-sucking insurance picked up the bill. 'And about time too,' might be muttered by anyone shelling out $25,000 a year, this being – for some – an annual wage. A national health service, such as Britain's, does not encourage similar thoughts and, according to my ex-GP friends, the sufferers from sleep apnoea and bronchiectasis within the UK are far less likely to experience the demanding regimens which partnered Nigel and Leigh when onboard the raft. We others admired their pluck in coming with us. We also wondered why they had wanted to do so.

Might either of them have preferred a vessel like the *Lady B*, this colossal craft coming alongside and keeping us company for a while near the beginning of our second voyage? Being forty-five metres long and with a mast reaching skywards for sixty-five metres, there was assuredly everything onboard that anyone could desire. One of its few passengers hailed us 'for a line', enabling goodies of various excellence to travel above the waves from them to us, such as New York papers, sliced turkey, a bottle of Chardonnay, cold drinks, suitable medicine for Nigel, and – causing shrieks of joy from Leigh – some of the stuff called ice. No sails were set on this temporary partner as we five rafters looked up at their passengers on deck and they all looked down at us. Was there envy on either side, with double beds more appreciated than modest bunks or for bunks than double beds? In the end, after mutual gazing, they drove off towards Florida, perhaps with important meetings to attend, schedules to keep or whatever the land could give which was not onboard her ladyship. We were slightly solemn afterwards, but the drinks and food were a treat.

The Caribbean islands near both of us were an extra-ordinary mix of unbelievable wealth and savage poverty. How astonishing it must have been in the old West Indian days, when the islands were up for European powers – or individuals – to grab, when pirates had their heydays, and ordinary sea-men surely revelled in the kind of life – palm trees, sandy beaches, exotic foods, sunshine every day and ladies of great variety – that tourism now provides. If one island proved unsatisfactory why not move on to another, to Grenada from Barbados, from Antigua to Guadeloupe. As a newcomer to the region, it so beset with intensities, I was also amazed by each island's shape and size. Cuba is not only much the biggest but many times Haiti, and Haiti with its adjoining Dominican Republic is many times Jamaica. Conversely, Turks and Caicos are minute, so too St Vincent, St Lucia, Barbuda and Anguilla. Puerto Rico is bigger than all four of those together and, yes, I did drool over the informative charts, lengthily and happily.

The only disadvantage with all these various hunks of land was their proximity. Some of them were very much in our way.

Most certainly another island loomed ominously some two weeks after our departure from St. M., when Sombrero was but a distant memory and which had never been so near. Known as Samana Cay, it lay straight ahead of us one night and was, in consequence, a great deal more worrying than its far-off predecessor. I therefore sat with the instruments, as was frequently my way, and watched to see what might happen and whether we might collide. Before too long Ali hurried into the cabin, said 'Rope!' and then vanished yet again. The American couple also entered, collected their life jackets and speedily disappeared into the outside darkness after saying that the rudder's fastening had become undone. This was serious, partly because the guaras had already been fracturing and were no longer so effective. To lose the oar, our principal guidance system, meant a loss of control that we had never previously experienced.

At one third of a mile distant we could certainly see Samana Cay and felt no joy in doing so. The chances were that reefs existed more on the island's eastern side, and that seemed to be the side which we were favouring. Water, of course, does not pass through islands and we would – presumably – go with the flow when reaching its dividing point. Most oddly, to my mind, we could not see the Yellowbrick positioning system which told everyone else – now once every four hours – of our actual locations. We knew our altitude and longitude from the GPS, but also knew there would be desperate anxiety from friends and other close associates who were following our track. They saw, with only those four hourly leaps to guide them, that collision was as good as certain. We seemed to be heading directly for that major hunk of rock.

Bruno, so I learned, was in the water and fixing our break with cord. Was he tied on, I wondered, and was some major

166

tragedy about to be enacted? I could have gone to take a look but, in cowardly fashion, stayed with the electronics. The others came and went, muttering morsels of information, and eventually one sodden Brazilian arrived to change his clothes.

'Fixed the oar,' he said, 'and we won't hit the reef.'

Even so, the Samana shape looked very close. We saw it from the eastern side and, despite considerable darkness, extremely clearly. I took no pleasure in the sight, but Bruno was elated.

'Now I go fix sail as everything good.'

Oh well, if he is pleased I might as well relax, although very much easier said than done.

15

Reef was not a word we had ever mentioned when travelling the Atlantic's width from east to west. There were no such things to be encountered. In fact there was nothing whatsoever to be encountered, save for wave, water and an ocean's emptiness, until meeting the West Indies. Reefs are frequent partners to these New World lumps of rock, either as modest adjuncts to the land or even bigger where they serve as formidable buttresses, being a major line of defence. Reefs may look enchanting, notably to scuba divers revelling in the beauty all about them, but they are terrifying to sailors of every kind. They can rip hulls apart in most straightforward fashion, their exquisite shapes and forms being much like razor-edged concrete waiting to destroy. In particular we knew that the island of Eleuthera, my longed for destination, was fringed all along its eastern side with coral. This was not continuous, as there were gaps between the bastions where twice-daily tides rush in and out, and somehow we would have to meet these entry points between ocean and dry land.

To fail and meet reef was a frightening prospect. Such a hurdle could assuredly kill, both the vessel and the five of us onboard. A reef had taken the life of de Bisschop when he and his crew had encountered one. Another had dismembered the famed *Kon-Tiki* when those six Scandinavians had come to the end of their lengthy voyaging. Their nine balsa logs were torn apart to arrive almost independently – before being patched up and eventually exhibited at a museum in Oslo. On reaching Eleuthera the *Anglo-Saxon*'s two survivors had, with most of their final energy, managed to manoeuvre between two reefs. In the book *Two Survived* which had so inspired me in 1942, its author Guy Pearce Jones had received facts from the men themselves and had then been most direct.

> Tapscott lay in the bow and directed their course. They threaded their way through patches of shoal and sharp rocky heads. It was easy to see them; the water was the clearest Tapscott had ever seen ... Twenty minutes later the bow of their boat grounded on the beach.

Surely it might not be quite so easy as those words suggested. What, for example, would happen if we arrived at night? Or when it was raining? Or the viz, as generally stated, was less than satisfactory.

A reef is not a recent creation. The thing may have been living (and dying) for tens of millions of years. Much of Eleuthera, as we later discovered, is formed of calcium carbonate, a limestone that used to be reef. Dig anywhere and very soon the spade encounters this form of rock, making human burial – for example – a difficult, or impossible, task. Out at sea the corals do not have everything their own way. They need warm water and sufficient sunlight, being unable to grow at depth or when solar radiation is inadequate. Reefs are also worn down by waves, by creatures that eat limestone and by the actual chemistry of the water in which they live. With ice ages coming and going, with land masses shifting, and bad times for reef survival following good, the shapes that remain to imperil sailors (for example) are the result of millions of years of change. What we might encounter in the year 2012 might have been growing and retreating long before human history was ever written down, much like grains of sand formed from coral so very long ago. All fascinating but, of course, irrelevant. The only importance was whether we would meet this living kind of rock or not, and whether we would survive any form of contact that was made.

Luckily, and skilfully, we missed the island of Samana Cay. The Yellowbrick brigade, as we called them, might have had kittens in watching its proximity, but we knew when we had passed it by and therefore relaxed when the island kept its distance from us – or rather when we managed to keep sufficiently distant from its solidity. Bruno was not in his element, in that he had never encountered such a situation, but he had become very swiftly adept at manoeuvring our craft. There is a lovely word in Brazilian Portuguese which is *jeito*. Basically it suggests something which fits the bill when the precise requirement does not exist. If you have only three spark plugs for a four-cylinder engine, what can you use to plug the all-important hole? If a fan belt is missing, and the particular item named N673b (or some such) is impossible to acquire, what can perform as that proper belt would do? Bruno loved visiting the upcountry regions of his nation, particularly its Pantanal, and he surely met that word, again and again, along with whatever problem had caused its use.

Therefore, or so I reasoned, he had a different approach to sailing our raft than straightforward yachtsmen might possess. He certainly rearranged our single sail, so straightforwardly used when blown by wind from our rear, as if it were quite a different rig. It almost resided fore and aft from time to time, thus helping in novel fashion with our directional ability. He invented new positioning for cleats, these being anchor points for any new arrangement. And he dug out the fabric acquired for serving as a rain catcher, this purpose never necessary as fresh water was not a problem. He draped this so that the cabin became less of a windbreak, it inevitably causing windage that we did not necessarily require. In short, he frequently broke rules without, in my opinion, ever knowing them.

Back at home, within the gross conurbation that is São Paulo, he ran a photography business in the area known as Brooklyn. It had five permanent employees and approximately 1,000 students, these many individuals experiencing some 800 hours of tuition every month with Bruno very much in charge. How to take good stills is the essence of Techimage, and fifteen teachers are there to help him. No wonder, then, that he spent much onboard time clicking away with cameras, with different lenses and certainly with different subject matter. Of course he showed us shots that he had taken in Antarctica, where he had been for several summer seasons, and in Brazil's upcountry states, where he could revel in their wildness. I did not understand, at first, how he could live in such a crowded city as São Paulo, with all its poverty and great wealth so intermingled, but his house did look most fine and was, I felt sure, untypical.

'It has fifty-three trees growing,' he proudly told.

That seemed to sum up the man, his place and his lifelong awareness of what – apart from family – meant most to him. How many owners of woodland properties know, to the nearest tree, how many are standing there?

Ali Porteous, the woman most able to help him when not filming, would also show pictures of her own piece of paradise, the 500-acre island that she had acquired – for modest price – within Uganda's bit of Lake Victoria. There had been no human inhabitants when she had acquired it, and she had turned the place into a supreme establishment for visitors coming to her adopted nation who wanted excellence – this coupled with fine beaches and good swimming opportunities either on or below the surface. It also had a perfect climate which helped to make it a great place for relaxation whether the sun was setting, rising or merely turning its devotees a different shade of brown. The principal building, with accommodation on either side of a central eating area, had been built by her. Proudly she told of making bricks, laying them and then enjoying their company. Later she realized that single-acre lots could also be sold to different kinds of visitor, to those who liked constructing their own dwellings as they thought fit in some region of the island which they most admired. Now she lives in the capital, Kampala, and busily starts up other businesses.

Her two children live mainly in the UK but both often return to the land and lifestyle where the two of them were raised. Bruno's children are much younger, one a mere babe and the other aged ten. As for his upbringing, Nigel often spoke of earlier days in what is now Zimbabwe and had in his day been Southern Rhodesia. Shooting with various kinds of weaponry had appealed to him, along with all the emptiness of that colossal nation. To be a boy in a land like that must leave its mark, however much subsequent living takes place most differently, as in suburban Boston. After being brutally sacked as architect he settled for teaching potential oarsmen and women how to row, this being for him a favoured sport.

We humans do have this form of ambivalence, particularly these days. For our earliest years we live lives in a manner thrust upon us and then, on leaving the nest, change to something much the same or entirely different. I was glad, when on the raft, to learn of these alternative existences along with their modern times. It was two for the price of one, as it were, with Nigel having a twelve-bore in his hands while roaming African emptiness and then the work he subsequently did concerning, in the main, a brand-new library. As for Leigh, I think there has been less change. She now runs a little company concerned with interior design but, on reflection, I cannot remember her telling tales about the times when she was young.

My introduction to Nigel had occurred shortly before he was even born. His parents were a great joy to me during student days at Oxford. His father was also Balliol whereas she, his wife, could be relied upon for cake, for biscuits, a charming smile and the comfort of a home. One day, having parked my bike, I rang the bell and was met by a tear-stained face. The nurse who had recently visited had apparently suggested that the developing foetus might be dead. I knew that she was pregnant, making her yet more feminine in my eyes, and was of course appalled. She promptly asked if I would listen and perhaps hear another heart beating within her bulge. With that she lifted up her dress to expose a great deal of unfamiliar territory. On which side of her to place an ear? Either I would then look upwards towards those breasts or – dread the thought – look downwards which was yet more worrying. When my perfunctory listening was concluded I assured her that another life still lived, although I was totally unaware that foetal heartbeat has quite a different style – all I had heard had been intestinal gurgling of great quantity. Her tears were brushed aside with my good news, and I was offered the role of godparent 'should the baby live'. On that evening so very long ago a doctor had confirmed my diagnosis and Nigel then duly arrived, some sixty-two years before he found himself sitting on a raft and in my company.

Being frighteningly aware of oxygen, and of its possible lack, must be a day-in, day-out concern. Couple with that an unpleasant reaction to the displeasing motion when at sea, and it was a greater puzzle why Nigel did not lie down, perhaps semi-permanently, upon his bunk. Instead, although walking slowly, he was good at lending a hand should a hand be helpful. He refused to be restrained merely because some problems were in his way. Or had once been, as I learned from a scar on his back, caused by treatment for spinal stenosis when three major operations had been necessary, these presumably recommended because insurance picked up the bill.

My two raft crews, I swiftly realized, were so wildly different. The first trio of Andy, Dave and John were by no means similar individuals but there was a uniformity quite missing among the foursome that then arrived. This was partly because a single gender had been replaced by mixed doubles (as tennis likes to phrase it), but the second lot was so varied by comparison with the first. I do not know how Bruno would have behaved if Dave had been in charge, or Ali would have done, but thought that the two from Boston might have stayed much the same. For my part I found the second trip more pleasing, the chat more wide-ranging and the dissimilar assembly so often taking me by surprise. I even managed – in time – to restrain some of my generalizations, particularly if they affected, or offended or ridiculed, the great US of A.

I had suspected the cabin might have been kept cleaner on the second leg, and so it was. I had suspected better cooking, and so it also was. I had not dreamed that bread could be made onboard to look like bread and taste like bread, as it did when Leigh followed a recipe to the letter. Indeed she liked to do things as near like home as possible, with dinner, for example, always sharp at 6 p.m. I was reminded of those 'mobile homes' which visit America's beauty spots in particular and also in great quantity. Are the actual homes of their owners as well stocked with gadgetry as the mobile kind? And are the wheeled conveyors a brand-new challenge, perhaps more important and exciting than the sights and experiences to be enjoyed near the parking lot? When Bill Bryson was on this subject he even mentioned solar-powered corkscrews – and I believed him until giving them an extra ounce of thought.

Where do all the modern 'essentials' come from anyway? Once upon a time we had no need for pop-up toasters, pressure cookers, microwaves, automatic kettles, pre-set ovens, plastic wrapping, ice creators and huge fridges in which even tins are stored. So what will be the next 'must have'? Somewhere, in a shack or gleaming laboratory, there are surely people creating new objects we will then have to buy. Devices to cool drinks down and prevent coffee scalding? Chemicals to change colours, making peas more pea-green than ever, along with apples rosier than when growing upon a tree? Or zapping nourishment in food so that we can eat, and eat, but not grow larger as a disturbing consequence? I suspected, perhaps wrongly, that Americans would hear of such an item down at the tennis club, and then would buy – along with the many millions of us following their lead.

On this second voyage we were not only less alone onboard but there were more big ships to be seen. *Ocean Express, Tropic Night* and *Carnival Destiny* all passed by, sometimes coming closer than necessary to inspect the modest blip (of us) observed on their radar screens. This particular threesome were tourist ships, multi-decked, multi-swimming-pooled, and multi-everything that money could buy and need. So what did their clientele think when gazing from Level 8 (or wherever) at the diminutive thing out there sharing their ocean space? Envy? Surely not. Concern? Perhaps. Curiosity? Quite possibly, when wondering what we did for entertainment, for booze and general conviviality. At all events they soon sheared off, leaving us curious to know if their loudspeaker systems had informed the 'guests' of our presence, much as whales might be sighted and then mentioned, as with approaching thunderstorms.

The raft was able to let us know what other people thought in quite a different manner. As with the previous trip, we could read each other's emails, either departing or arriving. With just one computer in use, and it handling all our traffic, it seemed fair game, much like reading postcards, to see what was going out and – a deal more fun – what was coming in.

The Bostonians' single daughter complained at 'all the talk about food', preferring to learn and understand what it was like upon a raft. I cannot remember reading, however sneakily, about clouds or sunsets or animals (like the squid propelled onboard) and other such happenings. It is perhaps silly to think of food as an addiction but I did wonder at its import-ance, certainly in the outgoing correspondence. We are 'now down to dog food', complained Leigh one day when meatballs were on the menu. In which case lucky dogs, I thought, being personally undisturbed about this fare. Bruno was seemingly and entirely unconcerned about all the platefuls put in front of him. He just tucked into them, ate them totally and that was that. If he was asked, perhaps two minutes later, what he had so recently consumed, I doubted if he'd know – or care. Nigel probably knew, even if – or particularly – the meal was then donated elsewhere. Leigh suspected, as I subsequently read, that the meatballs had done him harm.

Personal thoughts, of course, were never shared unless merrily donated. I was principal villain in believing that facts swirling within my head would entertain the others, and I often dared to speak them. One day it suddenly hit me that human males provide all the thrust for human evolution whereas our females do little of the kind. This is because the female eggs are made, as it were, in one go. By the third month of pregnancy the whole lot is assembled. This number is much reduced by the time of birth, and reduced yet again before puberty is reached. The diminishing is not important – although very weird – but the chance of a mutation being involved is much less likely than with males. Men make sperm, again and again and again, for all those ejaculations. Therefore mutations are much more possible with such fre-quent need for more creation. Every time sperm are made there is the possibility that some new mutation will have been forwarded. Of course only single spermatozoa achieve the

176

fertilization but, with dividing cells so relentlessly making sperm, the chances that a mutation is involved are far greater with men than women.

I liked such thoughts, even if my audience sometimes disbanded, choosing most disarmingly to do the washing-up. Never before, save on the raft, had I wondered why prey animals bothered to flee from predators. Why not just lie down and suffer the consequences? The small brains cannot contemplate the inevitable result, with unwelcome pain probably involved and then dismemberment. Nevertheless, every creature tries to flee. The answer has to be that the impulse to escape is inherited. It survives to a greater degree than the alternative of not caring to do so. At least, as I reflected sadly afterwards, the washing up had been performed satisfactorily. There is, most helpfully, often gain with loss.

16

It was no surprise when the second leg of our Atlantic voyaging became far trickier than the first, with navigation and direction producing problems of quite a different style. We certainly knew so after twenty-three days and when approaching the island long proclaimed – by me – as our destination. In theory, and according to wishful thinking, we should not have been able to see Eleuthera while attempting to head north. In practice that length of land was disturbingly visible when it existed only a mile or so away on our port side. The plan had been, bearing the prevailing north-east wind in mind (as already reported), to crab our way northwards as much as possible and then turn west for the desired island after reaching the appropriate latitude, with that particular parallel being the one to witness the arrival of those two British merchant sailors back in 1940. Our dream – my dream in particular – had been to meet the very beach where those young men had first reached solid land after their heroic voyage of seventy days.

Unfortunately the wind – the gale – blowing at us that April from the north-east had gradually become much too strong for crabbing northwards. In truth we had done well since our departure from Sint Maarten, in fact very well indeed with our platform of a raft. We had seen other islands, and had even sailed west of two of them, but of course it was good to be sailing east of Eleuthera and not colliding with it. Nevertheless, and after twenty-three days of sailing on this second leg, the longed-for island had become terribly conspicuous for being so very near.

It happened to be a Friday when things started to go so wrong. I thought back to David, telling us – quite often – of superstitions concerning Fridays when afloat, and that rabbits should never be mentioned, that crew should never whistle and ill fortune would always punish each transgression, and it was a Friday when the wind blew so strongly and nothing could be done to alter that disturbing fact.

We could see a few street lights on Eleuthera, plus the twin beams from several cars, and there was also the smudgy outline of the land itself. All wishes, and all hopes, of arriving at the 'sailors' beach' were very quickly banished. Instead we would head for the place named Governor's Harbour, this clearly detailed on the charts some thirty miles ahead of us. They also showed that the island bent more to the north-west, rather than straight north, a few miles further on from our expected route, this curious Bahama land a hundred miles in length and varying in width from two miles (where it narrowed) to six miles (at its broadest). Provided we could reach that turning point without encountering any piece of solid ground there should be no major difficulty – or rather less difficulty than if the island had continued directly to the north. Anyhow, we set off flares to tell others we were in trouble, knowing that help of some sort would be useful, particularly information. It was therefore occasion for opening up Channel 16, the radio frequency used by all vessels needing aid. It would undoubtedly be good to receive a tow into the security of that enticing harbour lying to the north and Bruno therefore spoke on our behalf to request formal help.

'Hello *Antiki*,' came an answer very speedily; 'On no account attempt to land from your present position. The reefs near you recently killed two men when they had difficulty with their yacht. The wind now is too strong to attempt a tow. We will wait until first light and then see what can be done. Over.'

This unhappy news was promptly partnered, as if to underline the message, by a strengthening of the wind. And that meant higher waves, along with an increase with our own anxieties. However much the other four onboard adjusted, tightened and altered the position of our sails, the land was slowly drawing nearer and that we did not like. It was therefore occasion to deploy our sea anchor and slow down our steady movement to the west. Darkness did not help, nor did the rain and certainly not the wind. I, with incompetent legs, stayed within the cabin and stared at the instruments. These were telling me what the others certainly knew, that the island was determinedly approaching however the sails were set. One of us held up the anemometer and it registered thirty knots. Such haste was far and away the strongest blow we had encountered – or rather which had encountered us. We had become its plaything and it did not care that ropes were being tightened, that cleats were being differently used, that Bruno and the others were scurrying from place to place, pulling, lifting, tying and grabbing in their determination to keep control.

Bruno eventually stated, and most straightforwardly, that he had 'lost it'. He and his helpers could no longer attach any flailing line to any of the cleats. In fact he, and they, could no longer do anything, save watch and take note of a worsening situation. The donated outboard engine might have provided some assistance but its choke was faulty and, after one brave effort, the thing failed to start again. Nothing like this helplessness had ever happened on the initial voyage. It also had not happened on this second leg, at least not until that storm had hit us, along with all the rain and water that it produced. It was now up to the fates to do whatever they wished, to turn us upside down or merely hurl us at the rocks. We each, most independently, confronted a possible termination of everything we knew. It was then that I was deluged with a potpourri of previously probable endings that had come my way. Why this should have happened I have no idea but everything was churning through my head in piecemeal fashion, a snippet here, another there, and nothing making any sense. The flickering reminiscences gave no comfort, in that I had survived those earlier bouts of mayhem, but my brain – or whatever now existed of my former self – was no longer making sense. It too had 'lost it', to borrow Bruno's phrase, and that was about all that I knew.

Suddenly, taking everyone by surprise, we stopped. It not only felt that way but the instruments confirmed the fact. Something must therefore have snagged our sea anchor; that was the only possibility. We had thought – we knew – that the surrounding ocean was sufficiently deep to prevent any such fouling, but the fact remained, as the GPS told so clearly, that we were as good as stationary. Perhaps some extremity of wreck was down there or an upstanding pinnacle of reef? Each struck us as incomprehensible but, no matter, we had stopped.

'Good,' said Bruno. 'We stay here and have sleep.'

With that he made a place for himself upon the cabin floor. Ali, Leigh and Nigel, all wet and generally exhausted, followed suit on the three available bunks. I, as worried as they were but not similarly dampened or sapped of energy, offered to continue watching the array of instruments in case anything should change. Just as frontline soldiers will do, should any relief come temporarily their way, Bruno was no sooner lying down than unconscious to the world. Beyond him, and via our cabin door, I could see Eleuthera's outline from time to time, with all those street lights and the car lights plus a fuzzy indication of the land itself. There was a half-moon up above but also too much cloud permitting any lunar brightness to assist those of us below. Instead there was merely terrific wind, horizontal rain, water on the deck and a situation the like of which neither our *Antiki* (nor its antikeers) had ever known.

There would be daylight in some eight hours and then perhaps a towing boat. Nothing had yet been damaged, as far as we could tell. The situation was not good but could, so very easily, have been a great deal worse. I shifted my back a little and felt a sense of relaxation not known for quite a while. The numbers on the GPS were so comforting. They oscillated slightly up and down but, on average, returned to give similar readings. It all looked so good and comforting. Magically we had found an anchorage out in the Atlantic. We would stay where we were until help might come with the arrival of another day.

But wait a bit – were the numbers still returning properly? No, they were doing nothing of the sort. New numbers were appearing and these could only mean one thing.

'Bruno, I think we're moving.'

He was up at once, and gave the shortest of glances at the instruments before hurrying through our cabin door. The other three then surfaced in a similarly speedy fashion, and also went outside where they took stock of what was becoming a desperate situation. Once again they slackened ropes, attended to cleats and tried to evade the flapping sail. I stayed with the instruments, these now augmented – via the clever software acquired from Sint Maarten – by close-up images on our computer screen. These showed our status absolutely. There was a small and boat-shaped outline representing the craft which was our home, much as miniature aircraft these days are often superimposed on helpful onboard aircraft maps to show lethargic progress through the sky, but there was nothing slow about *Antiki*'s jerky movements towards one reef in particular. I could even estimate how long, or short, might be the time before contact would be made.

'About another ten minutes,' I shouted, and did not hear a reply.

Two crew, perhaps Leigh and Nigel, were then on their knees attending to the small inflatable dinghy we had used on calmer days for taking outboard pictures of our raft. I could not see the point of their current labour but had no wish to interfere. Doing something rather than failing to catch ropes was plainly preferable, and I remembered David's oft-repeated dictum that 'you always step up into any form of life raft and never down'. In other words, stay on your bigger vessel until it becomes less satisfactory as a place to be than the far smaller alternative. The two crew members, hidden half-anonymously within their rough-weather clothing, were soon pumping air into the flaccid shape and doing very well. I stayed fixed upon our raft's progress towards that oh-so-visible line of reef.

'Another five minutes,' I called, more for the sake of calling than forming any service.

I now saw, slightly to the north of our position, some firmer shapes upon the screen more visible than the reef. These were plainly rocks, and sharply above the waterline. To encounter their general area would be yet more devastating than meeting coral. They formed a projecting buttress at the spot where Eleuthera turned more north-west than merely north, the kink in the island's outline that we had hoped to reach. Instead of being a more welcoming region it had now become yet more terrifying. No wonder, as a major switch, I wished that contact with the reef would hurry up, this so preferable to rock.

'One more minute,' I yelled, almost with exultation.

And then we hit. The noise – never encountered previously in any shape or form – was instantly recognisable for what it was. It was a groinching, this new word appropriate for quite a new experience. It was a grating, a distinctly angry and painful scratching, a sound and feel like none other. There was nothing smooth about it, and it continued jerkily. Occasionally the raft stopped but only, as it were, to gather strength for the next big forwards leap. And leap we steadily did, with more groinch, more grate and certainly more worry about possible damage being effected down below. Our pipes were strong – we each knew that – but what about the tautened lengths of webbing that had ratcheted them together? Were these being cut, sliced or somehow severed by the savage sharpness all around them, and by the ever-so-beautiful coral that is such a vicious form of living rock? Every day it has to withstand a battering from the sea, and it could so easily be taking revenge by resenting an unwelcome newcomer upon its fortress. Besides, how would we know of failure with those webbing straps? Would someone suddenly see a length – or two – of unhappy fabric, this flapping idly from below? Better not to look for it or expect to find the worst? And then we suddenly stopped without us banging any more.

Of course, of course, as we all realized simultaneously. The sea anchor! That had plainly snagged again, and most justifiably, with the reef on every side. I think it was Ali who found a knife and quickly cut the thing away. Too bad about the reef, with that great quantity of plastic material abandoned in its midst, but selfish urgency was now uppermost. It was almost pleasing to hear the batterings starting up again and I began to estimate how and when these leaps and bounds might eventually be concluded.

'Perhaps ten more minutes,' I muttered, not wishing to anger gods by being too presumptuous.

The radio voice we had received had been so utterly straightforward with its instruction not to attempt a landing in that vicinity. Petra, the beloved manager of Sint Maarten's yacht club, who had been inspirational with her assistance, had earlier sent a desperate message of advice that we were on 'a suicidal mission' if we persisted with our wish – with the wish, my wish – to reach Eleuthera. And yet here we were entirely disregarding these other people, moving headlong towards the island and in certain peril. Death would not be from anything self-inflicted, save that we had actually embarked, had done our best, and were now about to end within a reef. Suicide was not a valid word – the circumstance would do the killing.

'Another five,' I mouthed most silently, 'just another five.'

Still no flapping lengths of ratchet fabric. Still no single sign of dismemberment, but still the loathsome noises coming from below. Perhaps only two more minutes or perhaps just one. The little outline that was us on the computer screen moved so tortuously, but the leaps were still occurring which told us we were moving. Surely those very bangs were proof of progress. Surely, surely – and then great calm suddenly occurred. We were free and had left that living, rocky, spiky torture chamber. The surrounding waves, now diminished by that great length and width of coral, had been softened into gentleness and formed almost a caress. The beach lay straight ahead of us, plainly a thing of sand and therefore hardly to be feared. I still sat with all the instruments, loving their con-firmation of what I knew to be the case. We might have water washing over us when meeting the line where waves were breaking, but there was land ahead, lovely sandy land, and the trial would soon be done.

The end then came quickly. *Antiki* slewed round and water arrived from everywhere. We were heaved and pushed and then slowly edged further up the beach. There was seaweed on the shore – we were to join it, further flotsam from the sea. More heaving, more urging onwards, and then we came to rest. I clambered outside, received hugs and hands, and watched great joy in every face. Of course we all wished to dis-embark and the others man-handled me towards the edge. Standing would be difficult where the waves were coming to

their end and I gratefully accepted other arms and shoulders
to help me reach this destination. Someone brought my chair,
and there I soon sat above the high-tide mark to reflect upon
everything that had so recently occurred. We were all totally
undamaged and the raft looked great as well. Something
miraculous had happened. Another intensity had taken place,
perhaps the greatest of them all. What a day it had been! What
a twenty-four hours! And what would happen next?

17

Camerawoman Ali and navigator Bruno leaped about most of all and soon chose to run towards the car lights we had seen. Along with the rest of us they had been confined to the eighty square yards of wooden surface upon the raft and, with good legs beneath them, longed to exercise their sudden freedom. There was also purpose in their desire to meet some other people. It would be good to know precisely where we were and let the islanders know that all was well with us. Consequently, barefooted and happy as offspring on Day One of any seaside holiday, they vanished towards the headlights, these still flicking on and off.

The raft was steadily being nudged further and further up the beach, with each larger-than-average wave giving another heave. However it all seemed safe enough. When disembarking we had brought long ropes with us, hoping to prevent our astonishing floating home from going somewhere else. I assumed their weighty length on shore would serve as anchor, but Leigh and Nigel thought additional security would be beneficial. They therefore walked towards some scrubby vegetation, this lying above the high-tide mark, and bound some of its growth together with the rope leading from the raft.

I continued to sit upon what had become known as the captain's chair, and pondered the situation. It was extraordinary that the floating thing we had created during those few rushed weeks at Valle Gran Rey, this community existing on the Atlantic's other side, had survived not only a powerful storm but had landed us safely on a shore. More to the point it had travelled over the surface of a reef when on its way from one deep ocean to a very sandy beach. What other kind of craft could achieve such a happy ending? Certainly not any form of yacht burdened with a keel that surely would be swiftly smashed, along with a delicate hull, when meeting a brutal buttress of lethal reef. As for bigger vessels, their iron sides might survive encounter with rock or coral or mere sand, but they would be held fast by such a circumstance, and their crews could then only watch while destruction took its time. *Antiki*, with its pipes, its decking, its pig-ark of a shelter and its telegraph poles of mast and spar had triumphed, not smoothly, not endearingly, but certainly emphatically. I only had to turn my head, and there she was, resting on soft sand, now at peace, and with some 3,500 miles of travel in her wake. What a journey it had been! 'Old men *ought* to be explorers,' as Eliot said, and why not upon a raft?

Ali and Bruno then came back, most breathlessly, with a dozen or so Bahamians as happy company. Not even four-wheel-drive vehicles could travel on that sand, particularly on its upper portions of dune and widespread scrub, but no matter. The visitors just had to see what had brought us there and, along with great hugs of greeting, were giving amazing exultations about the craft now silent on the shore. The two police, also lavish with their enthusiasm (and hugs, a first in my experience), had seen our flares and had heard our talk by radio, but could not answer save by flashing car lights in our direction. I cannot remember anything said by anyone on that evening, but knew that it was good, whatever were the words they used. A house had allegedly been prepared for us, and an island's welcome would be happening as soon as possible. Eleuthera was overjoyed with what had taken place. We were not a couple of skin-and-bone shipwrecked mariners arriving in 1940. We were five enchanted individuals not really understanding what had occurred so very recently.

Somehow it was decided that Ali and I should stay onboard the raft, that Bruno would go to meet his family (who had flown up from Brazil), and Nigel and Leigh should enjoy the house placed at our disposal. (Nigel's seasickness had, alas, stayed with him to the very end and an immobile dwelling was, for him, particularly welcome.) Gradually the new arrivals all dispersed, and the two of us onboard settled down, like John and I beforehand, to talk in open fashion now that other ears had vanished elsewhere. Those on yachts, similarly confined although probably for less time, must know the tremendous and exciting joy of achieving freedom from close companionship which has lasted lengthily, perhaps for a month or more. Yes, Ali and I did talk – and talk – and were calling it a day when unaccustomed noises were heard as some people arrived to climb onboard. We were having company – and soon, laughing as she came, arrived the head of tourism for the island. With her were a couple of journalists and the night, I noticed, had just reached 2 a.m. Plainly Eleuthera has different working hours or was just curious. Of course all three visitors were great fun, with the larger than normal tourism official leading the show, and not one of them felt like going until 3.30 had arrived. More talk then between Ali and myself, still amazed at our so happy landing and no less amazed by everything since then but, eventually, we dozed.

For some reason, or none whatsoever, I thought the next arrival (appearing at 6 a.m.) was a beach cleaner. I certainly talked as if he was, and he behaved as if he might be, but Ali severely put me right (after an hour or so) when this curious individual, whatever he actually did – apart from greeting new arrivals on that beach – chose to go away. Eleuthera, long known only as a name, was filling in gaps about its style most speedily, and neither Ali nor I – however bleary-eyed – were displeased. After breakfast (of a sort) it was time for exploration. We knew our latitude and longitude, of course, for the GPS told us that, but not our whereabouts with reference to the arrival point of those two sailors at the furthest end of 1940's October month. We were not hard upon their heels but I wanted to know precisely where their heels had been those seventy-two years beforehand. Therefore, aided by a couple of solid assistants who had arrived, I set off – much like some drunk between two pals – from the raft to learn rather more about the island than a single silent portion of its high-tide zone. In particular I wished to visit James Cistern, whatever or wherever it was.

That had been the settlement, marked even on early maps, where a woman had dreamed of an interesting arrival upon the nearby beach. With this slimmest of reasons for his temporary banishment she had firmly despatched her husband from their James Cistern home.

'I believe there is something interesting to be found,' formed the essence of her thoughts and he, her man, departed, no doubt muttering as he went.

The nearby shoreline was some five miles long and, known as Pink Sand Beach, is normally quite deserted. Things were sometimes cast up there, such as rubber bales on better days, and the emptiness was often worth a search. It is 'finders keepers' on all that emptiness and there were those lucky days. Walking on its hinterland was difficult, with all the dunes and scrub, but fortune is a fickle friend and can be generous, provided of course that the searcher bothers to go and have a look.

I too staggered, and was assisted, through those same scrubby dunes but in the opposite direction. Eventually I and my two companions arrived at a clutch of four-wheel drives, this being their terminus with no further driving possible.

'James Cistern please,' I said to someone sitting casually in a driver's seat and offering me a place.

'You want James Cistern?'

Plainly more of Africa had survived than mere pigmentation, this being such a familiar style of reply over in the darkest continent. On that day, after many a lurch through sand and many a chat with passers-by, I was finally informed that James Cistern had arrived. It appeared to be more of a village than a town, but welcome whatever it was.

'Can we now find Garnett Thompson?'

'You want to find Garnett Thompson?'

'Yes please.'

He was the man, as I already knew from books, whose father had been a constable on that memorable October day in 1940. The parent had actually helped to retrieve the two emaciated men so suddenly arrived on his seaside patch. The father had often told this tale to his son and, with the older man recently deceased aged ninety-five, the son would therefore have to serve for me. Many a Thompson enquiry soon followed, with Garnett himself allegedly giving a helping hand at some nearby house construction – somewhere in that area. James Cistern itself, without any visible well or reservoir, proved to be a medley of fine and multi-coloured dwellings and, conversely, unlovely shacks devoid of occupants. Each chosen decoration was of a far from standard colouration, as if half-prices were guaranteed for the uncommon shades that paint distributors had been longing to dispense for many a previous year. As for the empty homes, no paint of whatever hue had come their way for a very long time, or ever, as was plain to see.

Suddenly a face appeared at the car window.

'I am Garnett Thompson,' it said.

'Are you Garnett Thompson?' I found myself replying.

'Yes, I am Garnett Thompson; I will take you to the beach.'

'You will take me to the beach?'

I was overjoyed with this new arrival and his all important news. Quickly we lurched back in our four-wheel drive towards the dunes, and there we disembarked. It was quite a hike thereafter, with many a stumble as I plus two new supporters followed Garnett, and I watched ahead of me as he settled down to wait beneath a wizened tree. This was a casuarina, as are most trees in that neighbourhood, and it looked extremely like the one which had sheltered the seamen and then the boat while it was being photographed. Incredulously, and after my arrival by his side, I heard Garnett insisting that both trees were the same, the one under which we now rested and the one the sailors had used when hoping for help to come their way.

'This is the same tree,' he said more than once, 'and this is the beach where they arrived.'

'The same tree and the same beach,' I repeated, echoing his lovely words.

Everything, so happily received, was suddenly unbelievable. There was our raft, perhaps a hundred yards away, and there were the two of us using shade provided by the self-same stunted and extremely ancient tree. Was someone or something playing games, with me in particular? Three thousand and five hundred miles distant, and at the Spanish community of Valle Gran Rey, I had solemnly declared to all who would listen that the sailors' beach was our choice of destination. Sixteen months later, immediately following a terrible storm causing us to lose control, the homemade raft they knew at VGR had groinched its way across a terrifying reef before coming to rest near the high-tide mark of a pink and sandy beach, this place previously encountered by two emaciated sailors barely possessing the energy to step ashore. It was all quite miraculous, and totally astonishing. It was certainly disarming for a very muddled individual, what with the loss of control and then the actual arrival spot. How could the fates be so beneficial and smile so perfectly at me? It still does not make sense and probably never will.

What also made little sense during that arrival time, whether we were still onboard, disembarking, running for the hell of it, hugging all in sight and then setting forth to discover Garnett, was our complete disregard of any film photography. During the first voyage I had filmed everything that I could, save that I had never filmed myself. Ali was on the second voyage, her principal task being to record all subsequent events, along with the man in charge. This she had done most actively. However, when the storm arrived, along with rain and during darkness, she knew the camera would suffer in such a wet and difficult environment. She was also, of course, aware of the general situation, of the plaything we had become among the waves, of the reef's audible resentment of our company, and she had frequently yelled with amazement at all the events which were taking place.

'Come on outside,' she had kept on telling me, 'you'll never see its like again.'

I, hypnotized by all the instruments, preferred to stay with them, and said so. But neither of us mentioned filming as something to be done. This gross omission is understandable, but was quite wrong. We should somehow – from the dry security of the cabin? – have filmed as best we could, with me telling how it was while glimpsing at the crazy world outside which had us in its grasp. Even when safe on land, and when running for the distant visitors became an option for those with legs, I only longed for proper legs myself so that I could keep them company. The wind was still strong, but the rain had stopped, and still we took no film. This was very, very wrong. When Sherpa Tenzing stood on top of Everest, and Edmund Hillary pictured him, the photograph was perfect proof of their achievement. Had their camera either been forgotten or unused the exploit would have been diminished in everyone else's eyes. This may seem silly but is true. Exultation can get in the way of the reason for excitement, as it certainly did with us. That consequence should not have been – but was.

Eleuthera lived up to its initial promise as a place of welcome. On the second evening after our arrival there was a huge party in 'our' house near Governor's Harbour. Everyone was asked for $25 on behalf of WaterAid and everybody promptly paid. They also had a great time and made us feel heroic. So too at the Rotary Club a couple of evenings later, and so too everywhere we went. We were taken on drives, visiting miles of magnificent and empty beaches, entering limestone caves, admiring the stately Cook's conifers, and eating or resting in shady places always possessing tremendous views of the sea. That island has three runways and is just 200 miles from Miami; so where was everybody? Oddly most moneyed visitors to Eleuthera favour one of its little islands only accessible by boat, where personal golf buggies are the principal forms of transport and where prices are nothing like those almost everywhere else. On Eleuthera there is a single road heading south (and north), with big homes hidden distantly on either side, with sandy driveways leading to them as connections with this so-named Queen's Highway serving as tarmac backbone for the island as a whole. It would be easy, very easy, we all suspected, to be very happy in this place. 'What price Acton?' I muttered to myself, many more times than once.

However there was still the problem of the raft. For a week it rested where it had landed, with the sea gradually urging it further up the beach. There was no need for ropes to hold it there, and the sea was treating it as it treats all flotsam; steadily pushing the stuff as far as it can on land. Of course the further our raft was pushed the harder would be the task of towing it to any kind of harbour, such as the massive and sheltered bay lying some thirty miles to the north; but, after a week had passed, and the storm had finally ended its energetic blowing, two fishing boats were able to bring *Antiki* to a safer anchorage, and that it where she rests right now.

She does not look much, being without a sail and somewhat lonely, but this construction of pipes, planks, mast and rigging had done what no other craft could do. The raft had not only travelled some 3,500 miles without any power source, save for current and for wind, but had then bounced for half an hour upon a reef before meeting a sandy shore. It had also brought its personnel in safety to quite another land, this being only one degree of longitude different from its starting place but forty latitude degrees further to the west. Along the way it had provided intensities of living, the like of which none of us onboard had ever previously experienced. In short, to borrow each frigate bird's specific name, it had done magnificently. Old men *ought* to be explorers and so should anyone wishing for intensity. That I had certainly learned as those days and weeks had passed by. I had been – as I had kept on saying and feeling – so very privileged.

Here and there did not matter; we had been still and still moving. There had been a deeper communion within the empty desolation. The wave did cry, and the wind did cry while we had experienced those vast waters. How did the famously poetic man know all that, he generally photographed in a severe, waistcoated suit while wandering around Bloomsbury during those creative earlier years of the twentieth century? As for one more intensity there had been loads of them; and that too he knew along with the rest of it. What a man, and also what a voyage for one oldish individual in particular, who was exploring as best he could and was then delighted to have done so. The whole business had been inspirational, over and over again.

Old men ought to be explorers. Now there's a thought.